Women in Ministry

England Evangelistic Ministries, Inc.

Mary Ann England

Women in Ministry

Taught by
Mary Ann England
"GLORY to GOD!"

Christian Literature & Artwork
A BOLD TRUTH Publication

Women in Ministry

ISBN 13: 978-0-9904376-2-8

BOLD TRUTH PUBLISHING
PO Box 742
Sapulpa, Oklahoma 74067
www.BoldTruthPublishing.com
boldtruthpublishing@yahoo.com

Printed in the USA.

Acknowlegements

I would FIRST like to thank God for the anointing He gave My Wife to Minister to hundreds, to thousands and now, possibly to millions about this subject.

SECOND, I want to thank Pat Harrison for asking Mary Ann to minister this in the F. C. F. Bible School, and for writing the 'Foreword' in this book. *(p. i)*

THIRD, a special thank you to Rev. Fred and Cookie Brothers for being my Pastors for 12 years, and for allowing me to minister to our church family at Father's House on several occasions.

FOURTH, recognition and thank you to Her mentor, Rev. Kenneth E. Hagin, for Her life-changing couple years at Rhema Bible School in Broken Arrow, Oklahoma.

FIFTH, as her husband; Charles R. England, I want to thank God for giving me the blessing and honor of loving, walking with, ministering beside and praying for Mary Ann England for 23 wonderful years in the Lord. *(See: 'My Life With Mary Ann' p. iii)*

SIXTH, a big thank you to all the minister friends that loved Her and stood with Her in Ministry; and prayed for Her daily, especially Rheba Peare, one of Her closest friends. They talked nearly everyday, praying for and uplifting each other in the Lord.

SEVENTH, I want to thank Aaron Jones of Bold Truth Publishing for all his hard work transforming Mary Ann's notes, references and teachings into book form; spending long hours editing, formatting and inserting God's Word into these lessons.

EIGHTETH, special recognition and gratitude to Loren Cunningham; David Joel Hamilton; and Janice Rogers, the Authors of "WHY NOT WOMEN?" This book deeply impacted Mary Ann, as she studied it (along with Her Bible) for hours preparing to teach these lessons at F. C. F.

NINETH, I want to thank both Dr. Chacha and his wife Regina from Martinsville, Virginia for introducing us to Kenya, for their fellowship, hospitality and hosting us for six more trips to Nairobi and Nakuru, Kenya, E. Africa.

Contents

Foreword

Our God is not a respecter of persons. Throughout history, He has appeared to whomever He wills and worked through whomever He wills. As the apostle Paul wrote in Romans 2:11 (NKJV), "For there is no partiality with God."

Though we have numerous examples in the Bible of women being used by God for His glory, there are still many in this world, including people in the Church, who treat women as second-class citizens. They can have babies, sing in the choir, play the piano, and teach children, but they aren't allowed to stand in the pulpit and function as an apostle, prophet, evangelist, pastor or teacher—just because they are female!

Mary Ann chose to obey God and preach His truth. Her courageous and Holy-Ghost anointed ministry that was accompanied with signs and wonders freed many, particularly women, from the bondage of false doctrine and the darkness of sin. Today, women around the world are fulfilling the call of God on their lives because of her ministry. Her legacy continues to speak through this book.

I thank God for the life and ministry of Mary Ann England. As an ordained minister for many years with our Faith Christian Fellowship family, she was a great blessing. I know that this book will inspire and encourage you to obey God, just as Mary Ann did.

Pat Harrison
Founder & President of FCF International

My Life with Mary Ann

I came to Tulsa to go to Rhema Bible School, not looking for a wife. I was single-minded to learn about God, not get married. I went to the 1983 Camp Meeting at the convention center in Tulsa before school started: while sitting on the floor of the convention center, I looked up and saw a beautiful Redhead woman. I tried not to look at Her, but as the week went by I kept seeing Her around the center, the first time I saw Her she was wearing a complete ivory outfit including shoes and hose; her red hair just stood out very, very dramatic.

I heard in my spirit, "That is going to be your wife what do you think?" I said to myself, "Shut up, I'm not looking for a wife, I came here to hear from God not the flesh." So I put it out of my mind, and the next day the minister called for all the ministers to come down to be prayed for, I was sitting on the aisle and when she walked by me I heard the same thing again. She walked down to the front and got prayed for and on the way back as she passed me I turned my hand sideways and her skirt flowed through my hand and again I heard, "She is going to be your wife what do you think?"

Two months went by and I had not seen her again, I thought it was over; no more thoughts of a wife. **BUT GOD,** and I am sure others have heard that before: but He absolutely put us together supernaturally.

My roommate and I were not satisfied with traveling all the way to North Tulsa for church on Sunday mornings, so we decided to go nearer where we lived. We found that David Ingles had started having church in Bob Yandian's church building on Memorial and 91st street, when Bob had moved to the Garnet location. So we went to church our second month at Rhema Bible school there was an aisle in the middle of sanctuary and I sat on the aisle, my roommate sat next to me. I was sitting there waiting for church to start, I felt a presence go by me and looked up and saw a redheaded woman go by me about 10 feet stop, look back, turned around and came and sat two seats from me. I thought she looks like someone I have seen before but I never thought she was the same woman at Camp Meeting. All through the service, all I could hear was, "There's your wife, what do you think?" Again I said to myself, "No way, I don't want a wife!" That voice kept saying, "Look at her she's going to be your wife, look at her."

So I looked and something changed inside of me, after church I would not let her out of the aisle: I blocked it and said to her, "Just who are you?" and she told me her name and that she was a minister. I thought okay that's all for me, again I am not looking to get married, so back to school and study The Word of God.

The next Sunday my roommate and I went back to Brother Ingles' church again, and I saw her again on the opposite side of the aisle with a man. I was so relieved, thinking she already had her a man - not me, Glory to God! But as soon as the service was over she hurried over to me to introduce to me her son, then I got the funny feeling again.

Time went on and we dated and she cooked for me and very soon we both decided we were made for each other, God showed me a railroad track, and the two rails going their own way and told me that we were like two tracks going separate ways and He was moving the tracks together so we would become one track: Same as in marriage where two become one.

She moved to O'Fallon, Illinois while I stayed in Broken Arrow, after four months I moved up to Illinois with her and we were married. We spent our honeymoon in the Branson, Missouri area in a condo. God provided all the money we needed and a new car to drive at the time. We began to travel around the state of Illinois holding meetings in restaurants, hotels and people's homes. We traveled all around the area, traveling to different churches and ministering The Word of God. We had two 'helps' ministries helping us and God put it on our hearts to get a sign over East St. Louis saying "Jesus is Lord over E. St. Louis."

In the mean time she got me to singing solo's in the meetings and we made a great team for the Lord, God moved through Her and ministered to hundreds of people in need, I have seen legs grow out; heart's healed; deaf ears opened; and many more miracles as we ministered around the country. Then we felt the urge to move back to Tulsa, Oklahoma: so we moved to Tulsa and stated ministering in churches in Tulsa. One church in North Tulsa, North Side Christian Church we ministered in every year and one year we held an Eight-Week Revival. God really moved for the people that needed a touch from Him.

About that time, Mary Ann met a African man, who invited Her to Kenya; we could not go the first year he asked us to go, but the next year, ... in August of 2001 we went to Kenya, (we both just really liked being in Africa) we even prayed and asked God if He would like us to move there. He never said yes so we just stayed in Broken Arrow Oklahoma and traveled to Kenya for the next seven years, ministering God's Word, Love and Power to the beautiful people there.

The first year we went to Africa women were not allowed on the platform, only men. But guess what, things changed. Where they had just wanted us to give to them, and women could not wear pants. By the time we stopped going to this place in Nakuru Kenya, Bishop Joseph Kama the people of Happy Church received the word from my wife and started doing The Word; giving to the ministers and others, and Mary Ann even wore nice dressy pants on the platform. We both loved the people of Africa

We loved each other so much, we always preferred the other before our self and life with MaryAnn was always peaceful and wonderful. Sometimes I would try to get upset with her for some stupid reason, but I could not walk across the room without God telling me to go ask forgiveness and hug and kiss my wife. I made it an ritual to never leave the house without kissing Her and hugging her and telling her I loved her. I never let her open the car door and never let her put gas in the car, that was my job. I also helped her with the housework (my job was to vacuum the house when it was clean up day) and I never let her mow the yard.

We were so close the we began to think alike, if I thought of going to a particular place she would say she was thinking the same thing, or she would say to me, "Let's do this or go here," and I really would be thinking the same thing. We grew together and life was just wonderful. We prayed together every morning and prayed for each other, every morning weather in the states in our home or in Africa, we always preferred the other and learned to talk to each other and learned to mutualy agree on things we did not agree on. The main thing was, we read The Word everyday and some months we would fast for a couple days, Glory to God!

GOD IS AWESOME!

CHARLES R ENGLAND

She was the love of my LIFE. My 'Shu chen,' my precious jewel.

I say 'was' because ...

SHE IS IN HEAVEN NOW FOREVER REJOICING AT THE FATHER'S FEET, EVER BEFORE HIS THRONE.

Notes:

Lesson 1

The Issue

"Why is the issue of Women In Ministry so divisive?"

Jesus is a lifter -Doesn't put down or under. *(See Gen 1:26, 2:18-20 3:16, John 8:31-32, Eph 2:10, Col 3: 10.)*

Some say the issue of women in ministry is the most divisive issue to confront the church since the reformation, Bible believing people are coming down on both sides of this argument, often with more heat than light in this discussion. Others try to ignore it, thinking it is not their battle, but a controversy between fringe elements.

The issue is hardly one involving a fringe element or a side concern. Its an issue that goes to the very heart of the church. When we look at this issue of women and their role, we are entering humanity's most ancient battleground the war of the serpent against the woman. There are several aspects of the serpent's strategy concerning women that we need to look at, together.

 # 1 The attack against the Gospel Workforce,

The devil knows his time is limited. He is doing everything he can to delay the completion of the great commission. One of his tactics is to simply cut the number of workers. Approximately 2/3 of all Bible believing Christians are women. When 2/3 of all Christians are excluded from the work of evangelizing, the loss for God's cause is so great that it can hardly be described.

Jesus said that we should open our eyes, look at the fields, and see that the harvest is plentiful but the workers are few. John

4:35, Matthew 9:37. Why would anyone look at the huge harvest we face, and the tiny work force trying to gather it in and seek to eliminate any workers whom God would call?

Matthew 9:37
Then saith he unto his disciples, The harvest truly is plenteous, but the labourers are few;

We don't need fewer workers. We need more! But the enemy is trying to cut back on the number of workers for the harvest in any way he can. I believe he is behind the confusion in the church about women and their active participation in ministry. And sadly some people are unknowingly part of this strategy as they allow tradition and the misunderstanding of certain scriptures to prevent or blunt the ministry of women.

 # 2 The attack against men and their ministries.

The temptation to keep women from obeying God's call on their lives is an attack on the males in the body of Christ. On the surface this attack appears to be only against women, but when we look deeper, it is also against men. How? The enemy appeals to the pride of men by saying that women are not their equal, not worth as much. Although some cultures call this attitude "macho" it is nothing more than pride.

The forces of darkness used Aristotle, Plato, and other ancient philosophers to spread the idea that women were inferior, even sub-human. This attitude was echoed by some JEWISH rabbis of ancient times who exchange the God-given equality of woman in the Garden of Eden for a view that gave women far less value. All of this appealed to the pride of man. The sin of pride is the refusal to accept who you really are. Pride enters in when you think you are better than others. It is the basis for racism, nationalism, and many other "isms". Pride is choosing to believe a lie about yourself. Pride can ultimately destroy you.

Lucifer fell from his place in heaven because of pride according to Isaiah 14. Now the devil attacks men through pride, by telling them that they are better than women. Because of some anatomical difference he tells them they can hold certain spiritual ministries that women cannot. Are all men leaders?

The results of this attack on men can be seen all over the world. Go into a church in Asia, Africa, Latin-America, Europe, North America, anywhere and you will find far more women than men.

The real prayer warriors, those on the cutting edge of intercessory prayer ministries worldwide, are usually women. Why? Because men have believed a lie that they are somehow spiritually superior to women. A man's pride destroys his intimacy with God and effectively stunts the growth of his ministry. Sometimes leaders have tried to bring better balance by appealing even more to male pride. The church has given special titles, status, attire, and money to men to lead congregations made up mostly of women. Also, the Body of Christ has elevated people who weren't ready for leadership, putting untried young males, over more spiritually capable women. Many are passed over year after year, even with outstanding leadership qualities.

When we begin to discover the revelation of God in this area, we will begin to free men to become who they were chosen to be, alongside women in spiritual strength and numbers. Our churches will then be balanced with men and women walking with God in positions of leadership.

 # 3 The attack against Women.

Ever since the Garden of Eden, when God told Satan that the seed of the woman would bruise his head, the devil has been ferociously attacking women all over the world. In countries based on biblical principles, however eroded, women fare much better than in those countries with little Christian heritage. But, even in Europe and North America women suffer more injustices than men. In the US women still earn approximately 74% of the salary men earn for the same job. Many of these women are struggling to support their children thanks to a spiraling divorce rate and "deadbeat dads" who don't pay child support.

• 400,000 teenage girls will become mother's this year in the US and will raise their babies without the help of the young men who fathered the child.

• 100,000 will be raped this year in the USA.

• Approximately 1 in every 3 girls is sexually abused before she grows to maturity.

• More than 800,000 women will be beaten by their husbands or boyfriends in America this year.

• More than 1,000 will not survive.

In countries with little Christian heritage, it becomes worse.

According to World Vision

• 450 million were physically impaired due to childhood malnutrition. (Allowed to only eat after men and boys.)

• Women are - ½ World's population, but own just 1% of its wealth. 70% of the 1.3 billion people living in poverty are women. A girl is twice as likely not to be educated as a boy.

• 2 million girls, mostly in Africa, and the Middle East, are mutilated through female circumcision to diminish their sexual desire. Little girls who survive the procedure grow up to face painful sex, possible infertility and a greater chance of dying during childbirth.

According to Time Magazine

• In Brazil, it is justifiable homicide to kill an unfaithful wife.

- In Russia, a woman's office job can include having to sleep with the boss

- In India husband and parents sometimes kill the bride freeing the young man to marry again for a second dowry.

Many women in North Africa and the Middle East have no identity. I read of an incident in a North African airport of a man dragging a young woman with a 6 ft cord tied around her waist, as he dragged her down the hall way of the airport, he yanked her behind him as if he were pulling a cow, yelling abuse at her. At least 40 people in the secured area including guards, paid no attention. No one gave the slightest sign that he was doing anything out of the ordinary. Had he purchased a wife or was this a glimpse of the international slave trade that though illegal, still exists?

In many Middle Eastern Nations women are covered head to toe and always silent. In some nations female rape victims are imprisoned for adultery while the attackers go free.

A New York Times' article with the title "100 million are missing" shows statistics that as many as 100 million little girls are missing in today's generation world wide, killed by their families because of their gender. In India and China mother's continually have abortions when they learn they are carrying a girl.

"Everyone wants a son, so they get an ultrasound test and if it's a girl they have an abortion... ultrasound has brought great joy." Other girl babies are carried to term and left outside to die of exposure. Another reason for the missing is neglect. If a son gets sick, parents will do whatever necessary, but little girls are often allowed to die.

The New York Times' article showed these missing girls are from populations of predominantly non-Christian countries. Even in very poor, but Christianized countries of Sub-Saharan

Africa, the Caribbean and Latin-America the number of females growing up with the males is normal. It is only the Countries with limited Christian Heritage that are slaughtering so many young babies because of gender.

 # 4 The attack against the Character of God

When bias against women is perpetuated by Christians, the message it sends is that God is unjust. When Christian leaders act unjustly, it reflects on the character of God. Unbelievers watch and decide that if Christians are like that, then God must also be unjust. After all, if God gives gifts to a person, then prohibits her from using them doesn't that make him unjust? Justice like judgment must begin at the house of God.

 # 5 The Attack against the Image of God

The devil is not only attacking the character of God but also doing all he can to destroy the image of God. He knows that male and female together are created in God's image. He attacks because he knows husbands and wives in unity portray the unity of the Trinity. Male and female relationships were broken in the Garden and since then the devil has been doing everything he can to heighten the conflict.

Satan is seeking to drive a wedge between men and women with the radical feminist movement, playing upon the hurt and rejection that women have suffered. Because females and males together complete the physical expression of God's image in humanity, the devil is promoting homosexuality and lesbianism. God gave us gender differences which we are to protect and rejoice in.

Many Christians fear women preachers because they associate such change with radical feminism. Some men think that the acceptance of women preachers is a spineless accommodation to feminism. However, the elimination of women from ministry is actually a sinful accommodation to a culture that isn't all that different from the male dominated Jewish Culture that Jesus came to blow up. Its not that feminism is affecting the church- it's the church which has allowed culture to rob it of Christ's redeeming work for women.

If young women involved in militant feminism were shown how radical Jesus was in the way He treated women, thousands would find him as their Savior and Redeemer, the source of the justice they seek.

When we look at these 5 attacks of the enemy, we could be discouraged. But, Jesus came to destroy the works of Satan.

I John 3:8b
...For this purpose the Son of God was manifested, that he might destroy the works of the devil.

Jesus came to restore God's original design and purpose for men and women.

JESUS PUT WOMEN IN THE SPOTLIGHT

In the three greatest events of Jesus' life, His birth, death, and resurrection, women were in the spotlight.

▶ His birth

The ancient world had a belief that the father was the only source of life for a baby. The woman was only the "soil" for the miniature human to grow in until birth. Of course, if you think of women as dirt, you'll treat them as dirt.

God took that idea and stood it on its head by having Jesus born with only a woman as His earthly parent. Think about it! Mary was the only human source for Jesus DNA.

▶ His Death

Jesus' death was the central reason He came to earth, His most important ministry. In the Old Testament, people were commissioned or ordained for ministry by the anointing of oil. Samuel's anointing of David was the outward sign of God's calling David to do something significant.

Who anointed Jesus? Who commissioned Him for His most significant ministry on earth? It was two women. Cousin John baptized him, but two women "ordained" Him. In the last week before His death, in Lazarus' home, Jesus was anointed by Mary. A few days later, another woman entered the house where Jesus was dining. She poured the entire contents of an alabaster jar containing expensive ointment on Him. She is spoken of everywhere the gospel is preached, Jesus put Her in the spotlight.

▶ His Resurrection

After the resurrection, Jesus again honored women, appearing first to Mary Magdalene. Women were the first to find the empty tomb, Jesus told them to go and tell His disciples that He was alive. So, women were the first to hear Jesus' command to "Go and Tell".

Women ministered alongside men during apostolic times, a fact we'll see plainly later. But, as the centuries went by, the church became more influenced by surrounding cultures than by the Word of God. It was only in unusual times of revival that women were again allowed the freedom to obey God in Ministry.

WOMEN IN REVIVAL MOVEMENTS

Historians say that in most spiritual awakenings, women were accepted as ministers in the early stages, often in the forefront. But later, as revival excitement cooled into organizational structure, the women were squeezed out.

The spiritual awakening that transformed England and America was led by George Whitefield and John and Charles Wesley in the late 1700's and the late 1800's. The Wesley Bro's had a remarkable, Godly mother, named Susanna. With nine children, Mrs. Wesley preached to more than two hundred people every week in a prayer meeting which she led in her husband's parish church. No wonder, John used women leaders for the small groups called "classes" which spread revival so effectively. Wesley said, "Since God uses women in the conversion of sinners, who am I to withstand God?"

In the early part of the 19th century, God again moved in America through Charles Finney, who invited women to pray and speak in public worship. Oberlin College which he started was the first college in America to allow women to study alongside men. It was also the first college to be integrated. Finney was the first Protestant leader to train women in theology. In 1853 one of his former students, Antoinette Brown became the first woman ordained in America.

Another evangelical leader of the 19th century, Dwight L Moody was eager to allow women to preach. Moody Bible Institute offered its Pastor's Course to women up until 1929.

Other moves of God saw women being released also. The Wesleyan Methodist Church ordained its first woman in 1863. General William Booth used women in preaching and leadership roles throughout the Salvation Army. The church of the Nazarene and other Holiness Churches starting up in the late 19th century also ordained women. After the Pentecostal Revival began on Azusa Street in L.A. in the early 20th century, several women preachers became well known. One of the many was Maria Woodworth-Etter who held some of the largest Evangelistic Crusades in America, until Her death in 1924. Another was Aimee Semple McPherson who founded the Foursquare

Church International.. God mightily used Kathryn Kuhlman during the Healing Revival and Charismatic Renewal.

WOMEN MISSIONARIES TAKING ON THE HARDEST JOBS

It was in missions however that women really began to shine, one man called it " burst of female energy".

By the beginning of the 20th century, there were 40 evangelical missionary organizations led by women. Armies of women missionaries went out, not only evangelizing, but also starting hospitals and schools. Women missionaries were the first to translate the Bible for hundreds of language groups in the most rugged, remote places. One writer said "the more difficult and dangerous the work, the higher the ratio of women to men."

When we look back to what Jesus did to release women and what the Holy Spirit has done in periods of revival, we must do everything in our power to release those whom God is calling today. We must all make sure that we are not part of the enemy's plan to weaken the workforce. When Jesus raised Lazarus from the dead his friend came out from the tomb alive, but still bound in the burial shroud. Jesus told those standing by to loose Him and let Him go free. Lazarus needed someone's help to free him. It has been 2,000 years since Jesus came to proclaim liberty to the captives.

It's time to set Gods women Free! From the human traditions and cultural ideas that tell them they cannot carry out the highest ministries of God's Kingdom.

Lesson 2

God's Plan

"God's Plan From the Beginning! Total Equality"

In the first three chapters of the Bible, man and woman are shown to have,

- A shared origin
- A shared destiny
- A shared tragedy
- A shared hope

Genesis 1:1-2 begins by emphasizing Who the Creator was. Then Genesis 1:3 through 2:3 gives us a broad panorama of what was created, starting with the non animate world, continuing with the animal world and concluding with humanity. Then Genesis 2:4-25 gives us a closer look, going back into the story to show <u>how</u> God created man and woman.

"It wasn't Paradise yet"

For the details of how God created us, Genesis 2:4 flashes back to the middle of the story, what happened on day six. God created the first man from the dust of the ground, just as he made all the animals.

Throughout the process of Creation, God had paused to give His opinion of what He had just made. Six times during the process of Creation, He had said "It is good". Then, in the middle of day six, He paused, looked at His handiwork and said, *"It is not good*". What brought out that negative reaction?

How could anything in Eden not be good? After all, God lavished the Garden with tall shade trees, sparkling brooks, green meadows dotted with red, blue, and yellow flowers, delicious fruit, even gold and precious stones. Yet, God looked at man standing there in the midst of this abundance and said, "It is not good for man to be alone." So, He created woman to be with man. Her arrival transformed Eden into Paradise. God gave His final approval, declaring that "It was very good."

A Shared Origin

To make sure that we would understand that man and woman were equally made in the divine image, God did not create Eve from the dust of the ground as He had Adam, or someone would have claimed females had a different origin-perhaps the pile of dirt God used for her was inferior to the one He used to ..make Adam. This would have made Eve somehow less than Adam, with her bearing less of the image of God.

God wanted to emphasize that both were made from the same substance. Eve would not be a separate creation, but a separate expression of the same creation. You might say Eve was the First human clone, but with a significant twist. God made Eve from "the rib He had taken out of man."

He reached down into the man's very core, took some of his DNA, adjusted it slightly, and made the first woman.

First Doesn't Mean Better

Can you believe some say that because Adam was made first, he is superior? That would make pigs and dogs superior to man, since they were created earlier. As the rabbis said, "If a man's mind becomes too proud, he may be reminded that the gnats preceded him in the order of creation." God's design for each of His created beings, not the sequence for their arrival, is what gives them value.

Serving Alongside, Not Underneath

The Bible says God designed a Help meet "a helper suitable for Him." Some use this to say that man was greater and woman was just his helper. But, lets take a look at this Hebrew phrase- 'ezer, a powerful word in the Hebrew. Think about when you were a kid and you needed help with a math problem. Did you go to someone smarter than you, or someone not as smart? What if you were having trouble with a bully? Did you seek help from someone bigger and stronger or someone smaller and weaker?

That is exactly what this Hebrew word 'ezer means. A helper is not a subservient peon, but a more capable, more powerful, more intelligent ally. It's the same word used throughout the O.T. when talking about God. Used 21x's & 16 are linked to God. The Psalmist used this word in Psalms 121.

Psalm 121:1-2
1. I will lift up mine eyes unto the hills, from whence cometh my help
2. My help come from the Lord

(Also: Deu 33:7, 26, 29; Ps 33:20, 70:5, 115:9-11, 146:5 and others)

The one who helps is the one who has something to offer the one who is helpless or needs help. Adam had no partner. God created a partner; a helper. How about the Holy Spirit, our Helper?

The second word of that phrase "k 'neged", shows what kind of partner God gave Adam. God qualified the powerful word 'ezer with the adjective "k 'neged", which means "equal". He made for Adam an equal helper. In Genesis 2:18, God gave man a help corresponding to him.... equal and adequate to himself.

Genesis 2:18
And the LORD God said, It is not good that the man should be alone; I will make him an help meet for him.

Woman was created, not to serve Adam, but to serve with Adam - to have dominion with him. If God hadn't added that word equal to the word helper, there might be questions about whether men could be leaders, too. Neither was superior to the other.

What was Adam's reaction when he laid eyes on woman? He broke into song Genesis 2;23. First human words we hear in Bible are a love song.

Genesis 2:23-25
23. And Adam said, This is now bone of my bones, and flesh of my flesh: she shall be called Woman, because she was taken out of Man.
24. Therefore shall a man leave his father and his mother, and shall cleave unto his wife: and they shall be one flesh.
25. And they were both naked, the man and his wife, and were not ashamed.

A Shared Destiny

God had a great destiny for men and women. When He first laid out His plans He said, "....and let <u>them</u> have dominion over all the earth".

Genesis 1:28
And God blessed them, and God said unto them, Be fruitful, and multiply, and replenish the earth, and subdue it: and have dominion over the fish of the sea, and over the fowl of the air, and over every living thing that moveth upon the earth.

That's shared leadership with global implications. As if to underline this, God then "blessed them" and said to them "Be fruitful, multiply, replenish the earth and subdue it". God's mandate was for both of them to rule. Adam realized that Eve was serving with him. We'll see, after sin, Adam said "The woman whom thou gavest to be with me." Adam did not say, "The woman thou gavest me."but said the one "to be with me." Eve was not his property, but his associate in government as well as his companion in the home.

The Romans clumped together their women slaves and horses, seeing them as possessions. What a different viewpoint the Bible has! We may look later at how Jewish scholars watered down the revelation before Jesus came. But, if we look only at the Word of God, we learn in its first chapters that leadership was given by God and had nothing to do with gender. God created man and woman and then shared some of His authority with them. Man and woman were going to join Him in ruling the world. What a heartbreak that they threw that away, surrendering their authority to the enemy of GOD.

A Shared Tragedy

The beauty of Genesis 1 and 2 was followed by the shared tragedy of Genesis 3. The telling and retelling of this story, has numbed us to its horror. We need to read it again. All the calamities that have broken God's heart and devastated people for thousands of years were bound up in those bites of fruit. Pain, torment, the twisting of nature, the perversion of humanity's gift; an in- calculable loss came when Adam and Eve turned their backs on God. They were enticed by the empty promise that they would "be like God". The irony was, they had already been created in the image of God and given the opportunity to rule with Him!

Something often overlooked is their apparent unity at the moment of their sin when the serpent spoke to the woman, he asked "Did God really say," "You shall not?" In English, you can refer to one or more than one. But, Hebrew has two different words; the you used here is plural. Eve also responded in plural, saying "We may....." The serpent's next words again used the plural you when he said, " You shall not surely die." Even though we only hear the words of the serpent and Eve, the text suggest that Adam was standing there, too, a silent accomplice in the crime. This becomes plain when, after taking a bite, Eve turned and "gave"some to her husband, who was with her, and he ate it.

Greek mythology says evil entered into the world through one woman, Pandora. But, it entered through a human couple. Both were present, both participated. Both were guilty before God, and both would suffer the consequences.

Those consequences included the destruction of male female relationships. Shame and blame, manipulation and control began. Both had thrown away their destiny. They couldn't undo the tragedy - they needed a Redeemer. God cursed only the serpent and the ground - the spiritual and natural worlds, God's words to Adam and Eve only told of the inevitable consequences of their decision. God wasn't putting anything on them. He was describing a future filled with sin. His words didn't declare His will for humanity! They merely described the inevitable results of sin in the lives of those who violated His will. Genesis 3:16 is a sorrowful description of the outcome of Adam and Eve's sin in the Garden of Eden.

Genesis 3:16-19
16. Unto the woman he said, I will greatly multiply thy sorrow and thy conception; in sorrow thou shalt bring forth children; and thy desire shall be to thy husband, and he shall rule over thee.

17. And unto Adam he said, Because thou hast hearkened unto the voice of thy wife, and hast eaten of the tree, of which I commanded thee, saying, Thou shalt not eat of it: cursed is the ground for thy sake; in sorrow shalt thou eat of it all the days of thy life;
18. Thorns also and thistles shall it bring forth to thee; and thou shalt eat the herb of the field;
19. In the sweat of thy face shalt thou eat bread, till thou return unto the ground; for out of it wast thou taken: for dust thou art, and unto dust shalt thou return.

Historians have distorted it, to try to prove that women should be subservient to men. But, the fruit of sin is never the will of God. Nowhere in the O.T. was there any divine command for wives to be in servitude to their husbands.

Nor, is poverty the will of God for mankind, but a result of the curse.

A Shared Hope

Right after the fall, came the first Messianic prophecy: A Redeemer would come! Jesus - the seed of woman - would restore hope to all their descendants. Speaking to the serpent, God said:

Genesis 3:15
"And I will put enmity between thee and the woman, and between thy seed and her seed; it shall bruise thy head, and thou shalt bruise his heel."

And He did! For men and women.

So, ask yourself "What then is God's absolute principle that should guide all of our thinking concerning men and women? It is equality. Absolute equality! What is modeled for us in the Godhead between God the Father, God the Son and God the Holy Spirit? Equality.

Deuteronomy 6:4
Hear, O Israel: The LORD our God is one LORD:

There is no hierarchy in the Trinity, only absolute equality. We are created in His image. Elohim - a plural unity - created man and woman in His image.... Equal.

Ruling together. Ministering together. And now,

Galatians 3:38
"There is neither Jew nor Greek, there is neither bond nor free, There is neither male nor female: for ye are all one in Christ Jesus."

"What is God's Absolute Regarding Gender"

What absolute is never contradicted in all of Scripture? Equality. Not just equality between men and women but equality between all people of every race, ethnic background, and class, between the haves and the have-nots, everyone.

Acts 10:34-35
34. Then Peter opened his mouth, and said, Of a truth I perceive that God is no respecter of persons:
35. But in every nation he that feareth him, and worketh righteousness, is accepted with him.

People contradicted this principle of equal value for all people very early in history. In the book of Genesis, people decided to build a tower. We still have tower builders today, but our towers are more subtle than the Tower of Babel. Our towers are hierarchies, pyramid charts, and structures that appear to give some people more value than others. Our hierarchical structures begin in pride and self assertion, not in God or His Word, and end in injustice.

Hierarchies are Greek and humanistic in origin. Even Satan's original temptation to the man and woman is Genesis 3 - "you will be like God" - suggested that they should assert and elevate themselves. We should all refuse this temptation. We all have equal value, even though we have unique personalities and different giftings, callings and functions.

Each of us is equally valuable before God. We should walk in this way, consciously copying the loving, humble pattern given us by the Trinity and backed up by the Word of GOD. Jesus taught us to wash one another's feet, to serve one another. This is the principle that should rule in the Body of Christ, as well as ministry: absolute equality of male and female.

Men and women were made in the image of God. Jesus paid the supreme price for both with His death on the cross. For God so loved the world, not just the males - that He gave His only begotten Son. Souls are souls. A male soul isn't more valuable that a female soul. A woman has absolute equality with men, in God's eyes; therefore she should be absolutely equal in the Church's eyes as well.

This is the only way man and woman can become one in spirit as they become one in flesh, in marriage. As we apply this principle in our churches, we will attain the unity Paul spoke of in Ephesians 4, becoming one faith and one body. This is when we will see the building up of the saints and the world affected for Christ and His Kingdom. God's absolute for all! Equality.

(See: John 17) They must see us as one.

Distorting the Image

The Old Testament tells the story of how God prepared the way for the woman's seed, the coming Messiah. In its pages we see a few people holding on to God's promise while most wandered farther and farther away from God's original design. We see very few respected women rising to their destiny in God.

As centuries passed, many Jews strayed from God's original call. Instead of the Jews spreading God's revelation and affecting their world, the world left its mark on them. The Jews were shaped more and more by the value of their pagan neighbors.

At the same time, other Jews built walls to protect their religious beliefs. They put the oral traditions of the Rabbis in the Mishanah. The Mishanah was obviously a document written for men by men. Men make rules for women, but women do not make rules for men.

(above) Mary Ann teaching 'Women in Ministry' at FCF Bible School. Tulsa, Oklahoma

(below) Preaching at Happy Church in Nakuru, Kenya, E. Africa

One of our ministry visits to Happy Church in Nakuru, Kenya.

Lesson 3

Women Leaders

"Women leaders in the Bible"

The Bible contains a rich record of women who were placed in authority by God. We must consider the way God used them before we attempt to pull an isolated Scripture out of context to build a doctrine that restricts the ministry opportunities of women. So, lets consider the following biblical women and the level of authority they were given.

• Miriam

There is no question that Moses' sister was considered a leader in ancient Israel.

This is confirmed in the Book of Micah.

Micah 6:4
"For I brought thee up out of the land of Egypt, and redeemed thee out of the house of servants (slavery). And I sent before thee Moses, Aaron and Miriam."

She represented the authority of God to the people in the same way Moses did. She spoke for God. That's why she is described in Exodus 15 as a prophetess.

Exodus 15:20a
And Miriam the prophetess, the sister of Aaron...

She is also the first person in the O.T. we see leading congregational worship. Oddly enough, many denominations today will not allow a woman to hold the position of Music Minister, Worship Leader and certainly never Pastor over Music Ministry even though Miriam was a forerunner for this vital ministry.

Miriam was truly allowed the privilege of authority and responsibility in ministry. But, is that something now forbidden or discouraged for women? Are women in ministry living out of divine order? Does the Word limit a woman's involvement in the church? Is a woman not qualified because of some "spiritual inferiority" to a man? Do you have an opinion, one way or another?

Miriam is first mentioned in Exodus 2:4, though not by name. *(Read Exodus 2:1-10)* Miriam is only 7-12 years old and already she has leadership qualities. Though she is not mentioned again until Moses had led the children of Israel out of bondage in Exodus 15. As recorded by Micah 6:4, we see she was apparently already highly regarded among God's people as a leader.

Miriam was truly anointed and gifted of God as a woman in ministry, she was a strong worship leader and a prophetess, raised up by God and inspired by God to speak forth His will in Exodus 15.

Exodus 15:20-21
20. And Miriam the prophetess, the sister of Aaron, took a timbrel in her hand; and all the women went out after her with timbrels and with dances.
21. And Miriam answered them, Sing ye to the LORD, for he hath triumphed gloriously; the horse and his rider hath he thrown into the sea.

She was fiercely loyal and extremely patriotic to the cause of the Israelite nation.

Gifting

Interestingly, the giftings of God can seem like a "two-edged sword" Those areas where one is gifted can be the same areas in which one is most prone to failure. One of the clearest instances of this is in the life of Miriam, She was a gifted leader and spokesperson, but she began to think that she was a qualified for more authority than God had given her. She not only thought, but she spoke. Numbers 12 records the account of Miriam's failure. She questioned the validity of Moses as God's spokes person.

What can we learn from Miriam's Ministry?

"We can learn something from everyone even if its what not to do."

The issue is the marriage of Moses to a non-Israelite, leading Miriam and Aaron to challenge the legitimacy of Moses as the mouthpiece of the Lord (v.1-3)...

Numbers 12:1-3
1. And Miriam and Aaron spake against Moses because of the Ethiopian woman whom he had married: for he had married an Ethiopian woman.
2. And they said, Hath the LORD indeed spoken only by Moses? hath he not spoken also by us? And the LORD heard it.
3. (Now the man Moses was very meek, above all the men which were upon the face of the earth.)

In verses 4-8, The Lord asserts that the status of Moses is above even the prophets and Miriam is stricken with leprosy...

Numbers 12:4-8
4. And the LORD spake suddenly unto Moses, and unto Aaron, and unto Miriam, Come out ye three unto the tabernacle of the congregation. And they three came out.
5. And the LORD came down in the pillar of the cloud, and stood in the door of the tabernacle, and called Aaron and Miriam: and they both came forth.

6. And he said, Hear now my words: If there be a prophet among you, I the LORD will make myself known unto him in a vision, and will speak unto him in a dream.
7. My servant Moses is not so, who is faithful in all mine house.
8. With him will I speak mouth to mouth, even apparently, and not in dark speeches; and the similitude of the LORD shall he behold: wherefore then were ye not afraid to speak against my servant Moses?

... and subsequently healed. *(9-15)*

Numbers 12:9-15
9. And the anger of the LORD was kindled against them; and he departed.
10. And the cloud departed from off the tabernacle; and, behold, Miriam became leprous, white as snow: and Aaron looked upon Miriam, and, behold, she was leprous.
11. And Aaron said unto Moses, Alas, my lord, I beseech thee, lay not the sin upon us, wherein we have done foolishly, and wherein we have sinned.
12. Let her not be as one dead, of whom the flesh is half consumed when he cometh out of his mother's womb.
13. And Moses cried unto the LORD, saying, Heal her now, O God, I beseech thee.
14. And the LORD said unto Moses, If her father had but spit in her face, should she not be ashamed seven days? let her be shut out from the camp seven days, and after that let her be received in again.
15. And Miriam was shut out from the camp seven days: and the people journeyed not till Miriam was brought in again.

Moses special status above other prophetic figures is emphasized. The Mosaic Law, then, is above critique from the prophets. So also today the Scriptures have a primary position over the prophetic gifts of the spirit.

• **Lesson: Do not talk against God's appointed leadership. It will bring His judgement and chastisement, and correction.**

The intent in v.2 is to legitimize Miriam and Aaron's right to criticize Moses as they did in v.1 (we see Miriam as a prophetess in Exodus 15:20. In Exodus 4 Aaron, as one through whom God spoke, where he speaks to Pharaoh for Moses.) In Numbers 12:4-8 God's revelation to Moses is unique. It is direct (plainly) and immediate (face to face). The clear lesson is that even prophets cannot presume to claim that their message is equal to that of Moses. (We have a more sure Word of Prophecy)

In 12:9-15 leprosy effects only Miriam, but it is important to note that Aaron is the one to confess the sin of both of them in verse 11. Verse 14 is the length of elapsed time prescribed for the priest's first and second inspections of leprosy in Leviticus 13.

The implication is that she was healed in response to Moses' prayer and would be pronounced clean after seven days.

(NOTE: Spitting in the face is a sign of contempt Deut. 25:9.)

Healing, Repentance and Humility.

This passage relates how Miriam was healed of leprosy. However, her healing was delayed seven days because of her sin of defying the God-given leadership of Moses.

Is it possible that delays in receiving answers to our prayers may sometimes be the result of a sinful attitude? Is there instruction in the fact that the whole camp was delayed until Miriam was restored? Repentance and humility will not earn healing, but they may, as with Miriam, clear the way for God's grace to be revealed more fully.

(Ref: Matt. 7:1-5; Ro. 14:4; I Cor. 4:3-4, 12:28; ll Cor. 10:7-18; Ja. 3, 4:1-12 (especially v.11-12); l Pet. 2: 1-3)

• Huldah

Israel had been experiencing fifty years of paganism when 8 yr. old King Josiah assumed the throne and at 18 rediscovered the Book of the Law, which had been hidden in the temple. When it was read aloud, he immediately repented and turned to the Lord, then sent his high priest, Hilkiah to seek out a faithful follower of God who could speak for Him. To whom did they turn? To Huldah, a prophetess who obviously had remained faithful to God during on of Israel's darkest periods in history.

> *II Kings 22:14*
> *So Hilkiah the priest, and Ahikam, and Achbor, and Shaphan, and Asahiah, went unto Huldah the prophetess, the wife of Shallum the son of Tikvah, the son of Harhas, keeper of the wardrobe; (now she dwelt in Jerusalem in the college;) and they communed with her.*

We know little about this woman except that she lived in Jerusalem with her husband, Shallum, and that her prophetic message to Josiah came true. The fact that Israel's high Priest Hilkiah, and his associates sought her out to make their inquiry of the Lord, shows that she had earned a reputation for hearing from God. It is interesting that a group of spiritual leaders operating under the Old Covenant in Israel, looked to an anointed woman of God for advice, when some leaders today, in the New Covenant age would consider Huldah "out of order" for assuming a place of influence in the church.

Prophetic Insight

Through Huldah's wise prophetic insight Josiah repented, staying God's judgement. This led to one of the greatest revivals is history. *(Read ll Kings 22:3-20)*

"The Woman and Today's Prophetic Possibilities" (Huldah) The name "Huldah" is derived from the Hebrew root *cheled,* which means "to guide swiftly." Perhaps Huldah's name reflects her quickness of mind and her ability to swiftly and rightly discern the things of God. In any case, the woman was used by God in this fleeting moment of history to voice His judgement and His prophecy and to spark one of the greatest national revivals in history. She is a case study of the character and the potential of a woman who will today receive the Holy Spirit's fullness and step through whatever open door God provides. It is worth observing how Hilkiah the high priest and Shaphan the scribe sought out Huldah for God's Word of Wisdom *(v.14).*

Clearly she had the complete respect and confidence of these men, a lesson in the truth that spiritual influence flows from a spiritual lifestyle and not merely from the presence of spiritual gifts. Acts 2:17, 18 promises that the church age allows for the proliferation of the Holy Spirit's anointing upon women.

Acts 2:17-18
17. And it shall come to pass in the last days, saith God, I will pour out of my Spirit upon all flesh: and your sons and your daughters shall prophesy, and your young men shall see visions, and your old men shall dream dreams:
18. And on my servants and on my handmaidens I will pour out in those days of my Spirit; and they shall prophesy:

Let Huldah's example of respectful trust, begetting, forthright living, teach the grounds for wise and effective spiritual ministry for all ministers.

• Esther

"We have to let go of who we've been in the past, to ever

move into our new season"

Romans 8:28
And we know that all things work together for good to those who love God, to those who are the called according to His purpose.

In the Greek, the word purpose "suggest a deliberate plan, a proposition, and advance plan an intention, a design."

God is at work to cause events and circumstances to ultimately conclude for the good of His people. And often He uses us, His people, as agents in that process. We are at those times, then, part of His advance plan, fulfilling His purpose through our lives.

Esther apparently understood that, for she allowed herself to be used mightily of God for the purpose of saving her people, the Jews from destruction. Let's look into the Word and find what it was about her that enabled God to use her for advancing His purpose. By studying Esther, we can learn much about fulfilling the purpose of God for our lives.

The name of God does not appear even once in the book, as is also true in the Song of Solomon; but His whispered presence and wise ways are constantly at work behind the scenes. His providence at work.

Spiritual Maturity

Esther's spiritual maturity is seen in her knowing to wait for God's timing to make her request to save her people and denounce Haman.

Esther 5:6
6. And the king said unto Esther at the banquet of wine, What is thy petition? and it shall be granted thee: and what is thy request? even to the half of the kingdom it shall be

performed.
7. Then answered Esther, and said, My petition and my request is;
8. If I have found favour in the sight of the king, and if it please the king to grant my petition, and to perform my request, let the king and Haman come to the banquet that I shall prepare for them, and I will do to morrow as the king hath said.

(Read also: Es. 7:3-6)

She feared God and not man. Esther risked her life for the sake of her people by going to the King without being summoned. She and Mordecai's mission was to save the lives the enemy planned to destroy *(Ref. 2:21-23, 4:1-17, 7:1-6, 8:3-6)*. As a result they led a nation into freedom, were honored by the King and given greater authority, privileges, and responsibilities.

Christ is Revealed

Queen Esther is similar to Jesus in several ways. She lived in submission, dependence and obedience to her God-given authorities Mordecai and the King, even as the Lord Jesus, during His earthly ministry, lived in total submission, dependence, and obedience to His Father God.

Esther also fully identified herself with her people and fasted for three days as she interceded to God on their behalf (4:16). Hebrews 2 :17 tell us that *"in all things He (Jesus) had to be made like His brethren that He might be a merciful and faithful High Priest."* As such, He both fasted and prayed for His own *(See: Matt.4:2; John 17:20)*.

Third, Esther gave up her right to live in order to save the nation from certain death, for this she was exalted by the King. In like fashion Jesus gave up His life that a world of sinners might be saved from eternal death and was highly exalted by God.

Philippians 2:5-11
5. Let this mind be in you, which was also in Christ Jesus:
6. Who, being in the form of God, thought it not robbery to be equal with God:
7. But made himself of no reputation, and took upon him the form of a servant, and was made in the likeness of men:
8. And being found in fashion as a man, he humbled himself, and became obedient unto death, even the death of the cross.
9. Wherefore God also hath highly exalted him, and given him a name which is above every name:
10. That at the name of Jesus every knee should bow, of things in heaven, and things in earth, and things under the earth;
11. And that every tongue should confess that Jesus Christ is Lord, to the glory of God the Father.

It was in losing her life that Esther actually found her purpose *(Ref: Matt. 16:25)*. She could have finessed and charmed her way into the place of personal safety through the King's favor *(Es. 5:3-6);* and indeed would have thwarted the purpose of God for her own life through selfish ambition or outright disobedience to what she knew was right to do.

Serve God to your utmost where He has placed you. God has given you to His Kingdom for today. As you let that be what guides your every deed and decision, you will fulfil His purpose for your life. We must partner with the purpose of God for His will to be done in and through our lives.

Positioned for Promotion because of Purpose.

"Rising to Meet Your Destiny" Esther was a Jewish orphan, a virtual non-entity, raised by her cousin Mordecai and with no particular promise. But the account contained in this book unfolds the way God opens destiny to any person who will keep his priorities. Even in the presence of recognition, success, wealth and luxury, an environment many may covet but which has so often proven destructive to spiritual commitment, Esther retained her sense of perspective and integrity. God grants seasons of favor for His people in order to extend His Kingdom. She seized her advantaged position to help God's people not for personal benefit.

Esther's Hebrew name was "Hadassah," which means "Myrtle," referring to the well-known and beautiful evergreen shrub. She reflected the myrtle in her courage and obedience, which clearly did not wither, even when she faced death!

In Persian "Esther" means "Star": again Esther's beauty, grace and character shown bright and unwavering against the darkness threatening the Jewish people.

NOTE: 1. Esther's response to Mordecai's call to recognize God's providence in her placement. She believed God, not her beauty, had put her on the throne *(Es. 4:14-16).*

• **2. Her respect for the power of prayer and fasting:** She recognized the reality of the Spiritual realm and the Holy Spirit's resources *(Es. 4:16).*

• **3. Her unswerving will to lay down her own life for others** and her practical good sense and patience in pursuing her enterprise *(Read ch. 5)*. God offers us a free will to choose or not to choose to partner with purpose.

Esther 4:16
Go, gather together all the Jews that are present in Shushan, and fast ye for me, and neither eat nor drink three days, night or day: I also and my maidens will fast likewise; and so will I go in unto the king, which is not according to the law: and if I perish, I perish.

"If I perish, I perish" sounds like Paul in Acts 21.

Acts 21:13
Then Paul answered, What mean ye to weep and to break mine heart? for I am ready not to be bound only, but also to die at Jerusalem for the name of the Lord Jesus.

(See also: Php. 1:20)

Ultimate Commitment.

"You do your part and I will do what you have said, even if I die doing it". What did she stand to lose, by laying aside her own dreams and desires to aid God's people? Her life. (Es. 4:16) She knew of only one source from which to draw the courage and strength to face the King uninvited. Though Esther's works are evident in her fasting and prayer v.16 demonstrates her firm faith in the mercy and providence of God. *(Ref: Ja. 2:17-18)*

Although she did not function in a place of ministry, Esther's life proves that God can and does use women in strategic positions of influence to further His purposes. Indeed, He singled out this young Jewish orphan and thrust her into the place of intercessor and deliverer. Her prayers and her courageous actions literally saved her people from genocide. (Complete extinction-Like Moses, Esther was a shy person. She was tempted to shrink back from her dangerous assignment but her cousin Mordecai warned her not to be a coward.

He told her...

Esther 4:14
For if thou altogether holdest thy peace at this time, then shall there enlargement and deliverance arise to the Jews from another place; but thou and thy father's house shall be destroyed: and who knoweth whether thou art come to the kingdom for such a time as this?

Many women today in the church have been called to act boldly and they, like Esther, struggle with fear. They are called to preach, and their words hold the power to bring deliverance to many. Yet how many men in our churches are willing to be like Mordecai to challenge these women to speak out? Some prefer that the women keep silent in the churches. But, is that what God wants?

Psalms 68:11 "This is a prophetic psalm. It is talking about the Good News, The Gospel, and the day in which we are living. It has troubled some of the opposers of the ministry of women to know that the Hebrew word translated "*company*" is feminine and not just a word of feminine gender, but a word which means women.

Psalm 68:11
The Lord gave the word: great was the company of those that published it.

Here is the way the Isaac Leeser translation from the original Hebrew reads:

Psalm 68:11 (Lesser)
The Lord gave (happy) tidings: they are published by the female messengers, a numerous host.

"After all, the first one to go tell, and to preach means to go tell the good tidings of the Resurrection of Jesus. Was a woman, Jesus told Mary Magdalene, "Go tell ..." and "They've been telling it ever since. And should keep on telling it"

- Bro Kenneth E Hagin
from his book 'The Woman Question'

Joel 2:28-29
28. And it shall come to pass afterward, that I will pour out my spirit upon all flesh; and your sons and your daughters shall prophesy, your old men shall dream dreams, your young men shall see visions:
29. And also upon the servants and upon the handmaids in

those days will I pour out my spirit.

This was fulfilled on the Day of Pentecost.

• Deborah

(Ref: Judges 4 and 5)

Among the Judges of Israel, Deborah was the only one who held the respected position of Prophet other than Samuel. She is referred to as a prophetess in Judges 4:4.

Judges 4:4
And Deborah, a prophetess, the wife of Lapidoth, she judged Israel at that time.

(As a judge, she held a recognized office of both national and spiritual leadership.) Her attentiveness to God's purpose and strategy resulted in an impressive military victory for Israel that secured peace for forty years. *(See: Judges 5:31.)* She was married but her husband, Lapidoth, did not share her position of spiritual authority, and we know little about him. Deborah functioned as a civil ruler and was so respected for her anointing and spiritual insight that Barak, Israel's military commander, refused to go to battle without her.

Judges 4:8
And Barak said unto her, If thou wilt go with me, then I will go: but if thou wilt not go with me, then I will not go.

We can see in the life of Deborah what allowed God to use her effectively.

'7 Basic Qualities of Leadership'

• 1. The Call

When we are first introduced to her in Judges 4:4, she was

fulfilling three specific roles (Her name means Honey Bee). Deborah had a definite calling from God, and He raised her up and enabled her to fulfill that call as she responded to His will. God calls us according to His own purpose and grace.

II Timothy 1:9
Who hath saved us, and called us with an holy calling, not according to our works, but according to his own purpose and grace, which was given us in Christ Jesus before the world began,

(See also: l Cor 1:26-29)

Don't ever think you don't have what it takes to be used by God. *(Read: Col. 1:15)*

- **2. The Commitment**

This is another attribute necessary for good leadership.

Deborah's ability to discern the mind and purposes of God was not something she could have acquired overnight. She had to spend time with God to become so wise. According to Judges 4:5, her commitment to the call was built on a solid foundation and grew stronger. She was disciplined. Because of the condition of the children of Israel, her role could not have been pleasant or easy!!! *(See: Matt. 25:21)*

Deborah was committed to the ways of the Lord, the people of the Lord, and most importantly the Lord God Himself.

ll Chronicles 16:9
For the eyes of the LORD run to and fro throughout the whole earth, to shew himself strong in the behalf of them whose heart is perfect toward him. Herein thou hast done foolishly: therefore from henceforth thou shalt have wars.

She was the kind of leader He's looking for ... not perfect, but a heart totally devoted to seeking Him. Loyal! She was a called and committed leader, but neither of those came without a willingness to embrace the cost.

- **3. The Cost**

Deborah was effective as a leader, but it could not have been without cost, she had to be uncompromisingly loyal and faithful to God, even while those around her were not. *(See: Judges 2:11-23)*

Some of the personal costs to Deborah in order to lead as she did, (Her marriage, her time, the culture, etc...)

Judges 4:5
And she dwelt under the palm tree of Deborah between Ramah and Bethel in mount Ephraim: and the children of Israel came up to her for judgment.

(See also: Judges 4:8-10; Php. 3:7-14)

The benefits of serving God by leading others far outweigh any loss.

II Corinthians 4:16-18
16. For which cause we faint not; but though our outward man perish, yet the inward man is renewed day by day.
17. For our light affliction, which is but for a moment, worketh for us a far more exceeding and eternal weight of glory;
18. While we look not at the things which are seen, but at the things which are not seen: for the things which are seen are temporal; but the things which are not seen are eternal.

(Study also: ll Cor. 11:23-12:10)

Leading others does require certain skills. Deborah's life shows us how to have...

• 4. The Capacity

God gifts each one of us with talents and abilities that He desires to infuse with His life and multiply for His glory *(Judges 4:6-7, 5:1)* Using these capacities to influence people for our own gain is called earthly wisdom in James 3:14-15.

James 3:14-15
14. But if ye have bitter envying and strife in your hearts, glory not, and lie not against the truth.
15. This wisdom descendeth not from above, but is earthly, sensual, devilish.

But he tells us using them for God's purposes is wisdom from above James 3:17.

James 3:17
But the wisdom that is from above is first pure, then peaceable, gentle, and easy to be intreated, full of mercy and good fruits, without partiality, and without hypocrisy.

How do we receive the kind of wisdom that allows our gifts to become effective for His sake? *(See: Proverbs 9:10; James 1:5).* Wisdom is knowing the truth and how to apply it. Understanding is knowledge seasoned and modified by wisdom and insight. Both come from knowing God; and that is also how we gain ...

• 5. The Confidence

We can read in Judges 4:6-7, 9-14 the effect her confidence had on Barak. Deborah's faith in God and confidence of His purpose was unswerving. That faith was evident to others.

Deborah was a bold and confident leader because of her relationship with God and what she knew He was capable of doing through a yielded vessel. She knew Him to be faithful and true and acted upon that confidence.

Judges 4:9-10
9. And she said, I will surely go with thee: notwithstanding the journey that thou takest shall not be for thine honour; for the LORD shall sell Sisera into the hand of a woman. And Deborah arose, and went with Barak to Kedesh.
10. And Barak called Zebulun and Naphtali to Kedesh; and he went up with ten thousand men at his feet: and Deborah went up with him.

(See also: Dan.11:32)

Another leadership-enhancing quality found in Deborah was....

- **6. The Courage**

Deborah and her people were up against a mighty foe in opposing Sisera.

Judges 4:3
And the children of Israel cried unto the LORD: for he had nine hundred chariots of iron; and twenty years he mightily oppressed the children of Israel.

He had 900 chariots of iron, commanded 100,000 troupes and for 20 years, he mightily oppressed the children of Israel. Her brave heart was willing to initiate action against the forces opposed to God's purposes for His people. She knew the spirit behind their mission was far greater than any opposition they would face.

I Samuel 17:47
And all this assembly shall know that the LORD saveth not with sword and spear: for the battle is the LORD'S, and he will give you into our hands.

Though she led the people in a actual battle, she had the courage to believe God would deliver the enemy into their hands, as He had promised. Deborah exhibited confidence and courage, born out of her commitment to God. She was a woman who had conviction.

- **7. The Conviction**

She trusted enough in God's Word, to act.

Judges 4:9
And she said, I will surely go with thee: notwithstanding the journey that thou takest shall not be for thine honour; for the LORD shall sell Sisera into the hand of a woman. And Deborah arose, and went with Barak to Kedesh.

So convinced of God's faithfulness she was willing to put herself on the line and her conviction was contagious!

Judges 4:14
And Deborah said unto Barak, Up; for this is the day in which the LORD hath delivered Sisera into thine hand: is not the LORD gone out before thee? So Barak went down from mount Tabor, and ten thousand men after him.

Her desire to see God's people free, stirred within them the courage to free themselves.

Final results - Jael took care of Sisera:

Judges 4:15-16
15. And the LORD discomfited Sisera, and all his chariots, and all his host, with the edge of the sword before Barak; so that Sisera lighted down off his chariot, and fled away on his feet.
16. But Barak pursued after the chariots, and after the host, unto Harosheth of the Gentiles: and all the host of Sisera fell upon the edge of the sword; and there was not a man left.

She too showed great conviction. She would have been highly rewarded for assisting the Canaanite commander, but instead she chose to act on the behalf of the Israelite Nation. Her loyalty was praised by Deborah in Judges 5:24. Radical actions were often necessary.

► **Judge:** One who judges, governs and passes down judgement, pronounces sentence, and decides matters. The root is *shaphat*, to "judge" "decide" and "pronounces sentence," In English, both "to judge" and "judgement" have negative associations, but not so in Hebrew.

Judgment is the balance, ethics, and wisdom, which if present in a ruler's mind enables him or her to govern equitably and to keep the land free from injustice. Judgement when used of God is the divine faculty whereby He runs the universe righteously, handing down decisions that will maintain or bring about a right state of affairs. Abraham described God as the Judge of the Whole earth.

Gen. 18:25c
... Shall not the Judge of all the earth do right?

In the book of Judges, God raised up human judges (shophtim) who governed Israel, executed justice, and handed down decisions.

Her Leader Traits

Deborah was one of these. (Study: *Judges 4:1-5:31)*

Godly leaders lead by inspiration. Deborah convinced her followers to extend themselves beyond their own vision. The inspirational leader provides a model of integrity and courage and sets a high standard of performance. He gives his followers autonomy and not only treats them as individuals, but encourages individualism. There is no better way to develop leadership than to give an individual a job involving responsibility and let him work at it.

Deborah did this with young Barak. She appointed him as her field commander and assigned him the task of recruiting an army to defeat Sisera. She was not afraid to set the example of courage and heroism by using herself as bait for the ambush.

"Deborah was a Multi-talented Woman".

Once again her name literally means "Bee" or "Honey Bee", reminding us of this woman's wisdom, how she liberally shared with her friends, and how her influence and authority were used by God to "sting" Israel's enemies. Her creative talents and leadership abilities distinguish her.

Deborah wrote songs and sang them (ch. 5), and she was a patriotic woman of God who judged (or led) Israel for 40 years. She might be called the first woman military commander and first Supreme Court Justice!

The keys to Deborah's effectiveness were her spiritual commitment and her walk with God, seen in the fact she is called a prophetess. She demonstrates the possibilities for any woman today, who will allow the Spirit of God to fill and form her life, developing her full capacities to shape the world around her.

The result of Deborah's skilled and anointed leadership is best summarized in Judges 5:31.

Judges 5:31
So let all thine enemies perish, O LORD: but let them that love him be as the sun when he goeth forth in his might. And the land had rest forty years.

We can't ignore the fact that the biblical record confirms her Godly leadership. We need more women and men like her today who will charge into the enemy's camp with faith and courage, willing to be led by God and to lead others for His glory.

In Nakuru, Kenya at Happy Church

Short Review

What Have We Learned?

The following is a short overview and questionnaire about what we have learned so far.

REVIEW

• **1.** To keep an open mind, setting aside any negative teaching you might have heard on this subject.

• **2.** To be prepared to accurately teach others what the Bible says on this subject.

Thereby, freeing both men and women in the Body of Christ.

There will be a final review and questionaire.

Overview of topics.

- God's plan from Genesis: Total Equality.

- How was the vision distorted?

- Women ministry leaders used by God in the Old Testament.

- Did Jesus believe women could be used in ministry?

- How Jesus broke down the walls for women.

- What about those often used arguments against Women in Ministry, based on I Corinthians 11, 14 and l Timothy 2?

- Paul's View of Women in the Ministry. New Testament accounts of Women in Ministry. Are women excluded from any office, according to the Word of God.

- Lies that both men and women have been told by the church, due to tradition and the misinterpretation of scripture.

QUESTIONNAIRE

►1. The enemy is behind the confusion in the church over women and their active participation in ministry, because he is trying to cutback on the number of workers for the harvest.

A. True
B. False

►2. Some say the issue of women in ministry is the most divisive issue to confront the church since the reformation.

A. True
B. False

►3. The enemy appeals to the pride of men by saying women are not their equals. Although some cultures call this attitude "macho" it is nothing more than pride.

A. True
B. False

►4. Pride enters in when you think you are better than others. It is the basis for racism, nationalism and many other "isms". Pride can ultimately destroy you. So this issue is an attack on men, as well as women.

A. True
B. False

►5. When Christian leaders act unjustly, it reflects on the character of God. After all, if God gives gifts to a person and then prohibits her from using them wouldn't that make Him appear unjust to unbelievers?

A. Yes
B. No

►6. Many Christians fear women preachers because they associate such change with radical feminism. It's not that feminism is affecting the church - it's the church which has allowed culture to rob it of Christ's redeeming work for women.

A. True
B. False

►7. Historians say that in most spiritual awakenings, women were accepted as ministers in the early stages, often in the forefront.

A. True
B. False

►8. God's design for each of His created beings not the sequence for their arrival, is what gives them value. Adam was not superior to Eve.

A. True
B. False

►9. In Hebrew, Helpmeet in Genesis 2:18: is 'ezer k'neged. 'Ezer means helper and is the same word used many times in the Old Testament when speaking of God. A helper is the one who has something to offer the one who is helpless or needs help. The second word of this phrase *'k'neged'* means equal. This shows us that God made Adam an equal helper. Neither was superior to the other.

A. True
B. False

►10. God had a great destiny for men and women. Both were created in His image and both were given dominion over all the earth. God's mandate was for both of them to rule as equals with shared leadership responsibilities.

A. True
B. False

►11. After their shared origin and shared destiny in Genesis 1 and 2, came their shared tragedy in Genesis 3. Both were guilty before God and both would suffer the consequences. Those consequences included the destruction of male-female relationships.

A. True
B. False

►12. Genesis 3:16 is a sorrowful description of the outcome of Adam & Eve's sin in the Garden of Eden. Even though historians have distorted it, to try to prove that women should be subservient to men, the fruit of sin is never the will of God. Nowhere in the Old Testament is there any divine command for wives to be in servitude to their husbands.

A. True
B. False

►13. What is God's "absolute" regarding gender? ___________

►14. In Micah 6:4, God told the Israelites "I brought thee up out of the land of Egypt, and redeemed thee out of the house of servants. I sent before thee Moses, Aaron and ________________."

►15. She represented the authority of God to the people in the same way Moses and Aaron did. In Exodus 15:20 she is described as a ________________ .

►16. Numbers 12 records the failure of Miriam. She tried to use her God - given position to legitimize her questioning the validity of Moses as God's spokesperson.

A. True
B. False

►17. The lesson we can learn from Miriam is that we all have the right to judge God's appointed leadership.

A. True
B. False

►18. Romans 14:4, Paul wrote "who art thou that _________ another man's servant? To his own master he standeth or falleth."

►19. When King Josiah asked his high priest to seek out a faithful follower of God who could speak for God, he went to Huldah a ________________ .

►20. Huldah was used by God in this fleeting moment in history to voice His judgement and prophecy and to spark one of the greatest national revivals in history.

A. True
B. False

►21. Among the Judges of Israel ____________ was the only one who held the position of Prophet other than Samuel.

►22. Deborah functioned as a civil ruler and was so respected for her spiritual insight that Barak, refused to go to battle without her.

A. True
B. False

►23. Deborah was willing to initiate action against the forces opposed to God's purposes for His people. She trusted enough in God's Word to act. Her courage and convictions were contagious and stirred within the people the courage to free themselves. Godly leaders lead by inspiration.

A. True
B. False

►24. Deborah might be called the first military commander and the first Supreme Court Justice, as well as Prophetess.

A. True
B. False

►25. The result of Deborah's skilled and anointed leadership is best summarized in Judges 5:31; "So the land had rest for forty years."

A. True
B. False

►26. By looking at Esther's life, we can learn how God positions us for promotion because of His divine purpose.

A. True
B. False

►27. Esther found __________ with the keeper of the women, which caused her to be promoted to the best place in the house.

►28. She also found ____________ with the King and became queen for God's purpose.

►29. Because she believed it was God's plan that had brought her to the Kingdom at that time, she was tempted to use her favor for selfish reasons.

A. True
B. False

►30. She was willing to lose her life to save her people the Jews from extinction. Her crises became her defining moment.

A. True
B. False

►31. The results of ________ and prayer can be seen in Esther's knowing to wait for God's timing to make request of the King to save her people's lives.

►32. Esther's life proves that God can and does use women in strategic places of influence to further His purposes. Her people were saved from extinction.

A. True
B. False

►33. As centuries passed, many Jews strayed from God's original call. The Jews were shaped more and more by the values of their pagan neighbors. But, God's revealed role for women was not distorted by the rabbi's teaching.

A. True

B. False

►34. Jesus came to set in motion the redemption God promised when Adam and Eve shared the great tragedy in the Garden of Eden. His mission was not gender biased; it was gender inclusive.

A. True

B. False

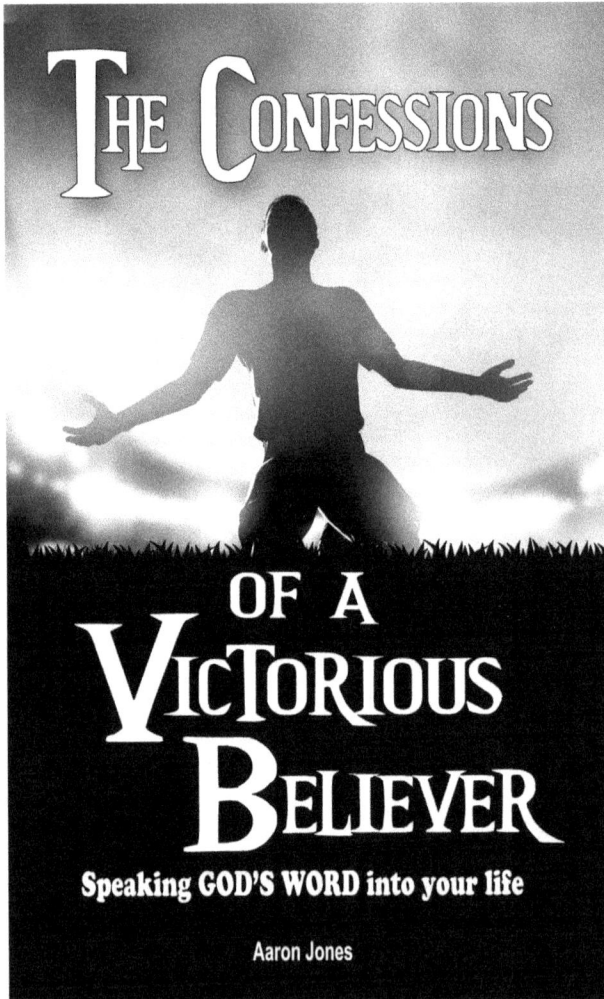

Lesson 4

Distorted

Before we go to the New Testament and the cultures both Jesus and Paul were sent into, we need to look at:

"How the Image was Distorted"

The Old Testament tells the story of how God prepared the way for the Woman's Seed, the coming Messiah. In its pages we see a few people holding on to God's promise, while most wandered farther and farther away from God's original design. We see very few respected women rising to their destiny in God: Miriam, Huldah, Deborah, Esther and others. As centuries passed, many Jews strayed from God's original call. Instead of the Jews spreading God's revelation and affecting their world, the world left its mark on them. The Jews were shaped more and more by the values of their pagan neighbors.

At the same time, other Jews built walls to protect their religious beliefs. They put the oral traditions of the rabbis in the Mishnah. The Mishnah was obviously a document written for men by men. Women were not offered a safe haven. God's revealed role for women was lost by both; by those who compromised with the dominant pagan culture and by those who tried to avoid the influence of the Greeks and Romans.

Men's interpretations of Scriptures regarding women seemed so forced that one must assume these scholars first held a bias against women and then imposed that attitude upon the words of Scripture. For instance, the Mishnah contained a long section with rules for women, Seder Nashim, but included nothing equal for men. It has been noted that "the absence of a corresponding section for men shows that in the patriarchies men make rules about women, but women do not make rules about men".... women ... occupy a marginal position, so far from God's original plan.

The rabbis didn't always agree with one another in either the Mishnah or the opinions that made up the Talmud. Their writings were filled with heated arguments that continued for generations. Some of these debates were about women. At times the arguments were based on the account in Genesis, and the value of women was upheld. More often, though, the rabbis strayed from the values shown in Genesis, they heaped scorn upon Eve, claiming that the serpent had sex with her, and this had "infused her with lust." Although Genesis showed the absolute unity between men and women, the rabbis distorted the image.

Devaluing Women

The rabbis read their own cultural values into Scripture, rather than look at God's Word and form cultural values from it. They said "Compared with Adam, Eve was like a monkey to a human being. Their belief in male superiority shaped their teaching, as shown by the following examples:

- "A man must be saved alive sooner than a woman, and his lost property must be restored sooner than hers."

- "Though a man has the exclusive right to his wife's sexuality, the wife's right to the husband's sexual function is never exclusive. She cannot legally preclude her husband from taking additional wives or having sexual relations with unmarried women."

- "Women are gluttonous."

- "Women are of unstable temperament."

• "Woe to him who has female children! A daughter is like a trap for her father ...when she is small he fears that she might be seduced; when she is a maiden, that she become promiscuous; when she matures, that she might not marry; when she marries- that she might not produce children; when she grows old, that she would practice witchcraft."

Women More Sinful Than Men

Contrary to the teaching of Scripture, the rabbis said that woman is more prone to sin that man. "For evil are women, my children ... the angel of the Lord told me, and taught me, that women are overcome by the spirit of fornication more than men." That's why so many of the rabbi's laws concentrated on controlling women's supposed natural bent to lust.

The "Bleeding Pharisees"

Everything about the female body was considered sexual. The rabbis said, "If one gazes at the little finger of a woman, it is as if he gazed at her secret place!" Women were held accountable, not only for their own sins, but also for the lust they awakened in men.

Like the Greeks, the rabbis believed that women were possessions to be used or, better yet avoided altogether. If possible, one should not look at or talk to a woman. One class of Pharisees was called the "Bleeding Pharisees" because they often ran into things while walking with their eyes shut to keep from seeing a woman. They praised one man who locked his wife inside every time he went out.

Rare Praise

It would be unfair to say that all the rabbis teaching about women was negative. Some occasionally said positive things. One who supported the value of women was Gamaliel, Paul's mentor, who likened women to a "golden pitcher." Another rabbi praised his mother beautifully. Whenever he heard his mother's foot steps, he said, "I will arise before the approaching Shechinah" (a Hebrew word for the glory of God). The reason a rabbi praising a woman stands out is that it was so rare! Sometimes even their attempt at praise showed that rabbi's thought of women as possessions; heart warming possessions, put possessions nonetheless. Many of their laws categorized wives together with slaves, cattle and other "possessions."

This is why it was easy for a man to divorce his wife, but not the other way around. As one writer said, "Whereas an owner can give up his property, property cannot abandon its owner. Even if a man became insane a woman was chained to him for life.

The rabbis disagreed as to what constituted "righteous" grounds for a man to discard his wife. They tried to draw Jesus into this argument, but he refused to take sides. Instead He pointed them back to Genesis, quoting God's original purpose for marriage:

> *Matthew 19:5-6*
> *5. And said, For this cause shall a man leave father and mother, and shall cleave to his wife: and they twain shall be one flesh?*
> *6. Wherefore they are no more twain, but one flesh. What therefore God hath joined together, let not man put asunder.*

> *Mark 10:7-9*
> *7. For this cause shall a man leave his father and mother, and cleave to his wife;*
> *8. And they twain shall be one flesh: so then they are no more twain, but one flesh.*
> *9. What therefore God hath joined together, let not man put asunder.*

Cultural Blinders

Jesus words did far more than discourage divorce. They elevated woman to God's original intentions: equality with man. His words stood in stark contrast to those of the rabbis who so distorted God's simple revelation. (But the religious teachers had cultural blinders on them that kept them from seeing the truth: that women were created in the image of God, just as man had been.) Because they denied that simple truth, they had to erect elaborate explanations, applying different laws to men and women.

We may marvel that the Jews had the Word of God and yet were so blind to the truth. But have we done differently in the church? Haven't some made categories of whom God could use and how? We can only wonder at what Jesus would say if He were to come today and confront cultural differences in the church.

Building Walls God Never Intended.

What an irony that in their zeal to protect Judaism from the pollution around them, the rabbis ended up with such unscriptural teaching. Their opinion of women was more similar to their pagan neighbors than to that which God had revealed in Genesis.

Jewish women were marginalized from the worship of God. They couldn't participate in many of the most important rituals. They were segregated into a separate court in Herod's temple, even though this was not part of God's original design for the tabernacle, nor was it the case in Solomon's temple, nor in the temple rebuilt by the exiles returning from Babylon.

As is so often the case, art followed belief. The rabbis had built walls of teaching that divided people. Now the architects of Herod's temple made those walls literal, with separate courts dividing Gentiles from Jews, the Jewish women from Jewish men. The architecture underlined what the architects believed:

some were allowed closer access to God than others. The rabbis of the Mishnah had compromised so much that they actually praised the design of a godless King instead of seeing how radically Herod had distorted God's design.

Women Don't Count

Most Jews could come to the temple, only a few times a year for special celebrations. Weekly worship took place in the synagogue. By the second century after Christ, archaeology suggests that the synagogues kept women in screened second floor galleries, that they entered by a back door. The rabbis decreed that a synagogue could be established wherever there was a quorum of ten men. Even though there was no basis in Scripture for this, they were sending a clear message to their women: "You (quite literally!) do not count."

An important public celebration of Judaism was the public reading of the Torah (the first five books of the Old Testament). Even in this a woman was usually excluded. The rabbis said that the reading of the Torah by a woman would dishonor the community. Women were also discouraged from the private study of the Torah, despite the fact that this was their closest tie to God, their highest form of worship.

The rabbis said, "Happy is he who was brought up in the Torah and whose labor was in the Torah." If that's true, then the flip side is also true; Unhappy is she who was not brought up in the Torah!

Most rabbis would not think of teaching the Torah to a woman. Rabbis such as Gamaliel, Paul's mentor, who taught his daughter, were the rare exception. Every young boy was required to study the law. It was the primary way to gain merit before God, but the Tosefta said that women were "not obligated." This clearly communicated to women that they had no real value. The rabbis taught that to be in right relationship with God, you had to observe the Law He gave Moses at Sinai. Yet that Law was binding only on free adult males. Therefore, no children, no slaves, and no women could serve God fully.

Boys grew up to be men. Even a male slave had the possibility of becoming a free man. But women could never have the same relationship with God as men had. The rabbis told women to earn God's favor by making sure their sons and husbands went to the "house of study," the rabbinic academy. A woman had to reach her spiritual destiny through others, she was always one step removed from God, even in the privacy of her home.

Luke 11:27-28
27. And it came to pass, as he spake these things, a certain woman of the company lifted up her voice, and said unto him, Blessed is the womb that bare thee, and the paps which thou hast sucked.
28. But he said, Yea rather, blessed are they that hear the word of God, and keep it.

Though some rabbis believed that God endowed women with more understanding than men, they did nothing to encourage women's spiritual or intellectual development. When they said that women "were not obligated" to study the Law, they made women "peripheral Jews." In the words of one, "An ignoramus cannot be a saint." Teaching a girl the laws of God was considered a waste of time-or even worse. Rabbi Eliezer said, "If any man gives his daughter the Law it is as though he taught her lechery. "Similarly the Jerusalem Talmud states, "Let the words of Torah be burned up, but let them not be delivered to women."

The Deepening Darkness

Someone has said you can't hear the good news until you've really heard the bad news. Put in another way, a candle never seems brighter than when held in pitch darkness. So before we turn to Jesus and His message of hope and freedom, we must look at one more arena of the darkness He came to penetrate.

While the rabbis were trying to build walls around Judaism, others were enthusiastically building bridges, linking their Jewish heritage with that of the Greeks and Romans. One of the best known of these was Philo of Alexandria, who lived during the time of Jesus.

The Hatred of Women

Philo loved Greek culture, so it shouldn't surprise us that he joined the Greeks in their hatred of women. Using Greek philosophy on one hand and his reinterpretation of Scripture on the other, he poured contempt on all women. He said woman "was the beginning of evil." "The female sex wasn't just weaker, it was more wicked, more easily deceived, and more prone to deceive. Echoing Aristotle, he stated firmly that "the male is more perfect than the female." Therefore, "it was fitting that man should rule over immortality and everything good, but women over death and everything vile."

Bending God's Word

To support this unbiblical view Philo pulled Scripture out of context. Instead of allowing the Word to shine light on his cultural beliefs, he bent the Word to serve his beliefs. Instead of presenting Genesis 3:16 as the sorrowful description of the outcome of Adam and Eve's sin in the Garden of Eden, he distorted the verse to try to prove that God's will was that women be subservient to men.

Genesis 3:16-19
16. Unto the woman he said, I will greatly multiply thy sorrow and thy conception; in sorrow thou shalt bring forth children; and thy desire shall be to thy husband, and he

shall rule over thee.
17. And unto Adam he said, Because thou hast hearkened unto the voice of thy wife, and hast eaten of the tree, of which I commanded thee, saying, Thou shalt not eat of it: cursed is the ground for thy sake; in sorrow shalt thou eat of it all the days of thy life;
18. Thorns also and thistles shall it bring forth to thee; and thou shalt eat the herb of the field;
19. In the sweat of thy face shalt thou eat bread, till thou return unto the ground; for out of it wast thou taken: for dust thou art, and unto dust shalt thou return.

But the fruit of sin is never the will of God! Nowhere in the Old Testament was there any divine command for wives to be in servitude to their husbands.

Since by his foundational ideas women couldn't be anything but evil, how did Philo account for women of virtue in the Old Testament? He did so with a stretch of logic, that would be comical if it weren't so tragic. For to Philo, the idea of "a virtuous female" was a contradiction in terms. The very word virtue comes from the word manly in both Latin and Greek. To prove his point, Philo quoted a phrase in *Genesis 18:11; "Sarah was past the age of childbearing."* The original Hebrew literally said *"There ceased to be to Sarah the ways of women."* He used this to explain the impossible. Sarah was virtuous because after menopause she had inwardly become a man. He said no other explanation was possible for the female nature was "irrational and akin to bestial passions, fear, sorrow, pleasure and desire, from which ensue incurable weaknesses and indescribable diseases."

There is nothing so foolish as an intelligent man using his mental gifts to explain away the simplicity of truth.

Philo wasn't the only one who tried to combine Judaism with

the prevailing philosophies of the day. Josephus, a Jewish historian, did so, as did a writer of the Apocrypha named Sirach. Sirach abandoned the biblical concept of shared responsibility for the Fall and placed all the blame on Eve: "From a woman did sin originate, and because of her we all must die." He also said "Do not....sit in the midst of women; for from garments comes the moth, and from a woman comes woman's wickedness. Better is the wickedness of a man than a woman who does good; and it is a woman who brings shame and disgrace."

How shocking! What a contradiction to the Scriptures that teach, *"The soul that sinneth, it shall die." (Ezekiel 18:4,20)* No mention was made of gender, for this is equally true for both men and women. The soul of whoever does the sinning will die.

Paul affirmed God's revealed truth, saying,

Romans 3:22b-24
"There is no difference, for all have sinned and come short of the glory of God; Being justified freely by His grace through the redemption that is in Christ Jesus."

Standing against what nearly everyone in his time believed, Paul declared the truth with echoes from the first three chapters of Genesis: Men and women have a shared origin, a shared destiny, a shared tragedy, and a shared hope.

Jesus Broke Down the Walls

Jesus came to set in motion the healing God had promised when Adam and Eve shared the great tragedy in the Garden. He came to end the painful consequences of a broken and sinful world, including the rift between men and women. Jesus came to set men and women free. But, because of the terrible exclusion that women had suffered, His open welcome meant even more to them. Jesus did not start a movement for women, but a movement for humans. It is not surprising, however, that women were especially responsive to His ideas. They were trapped in a hostile world.

Jesus' mission wasn't gender biased; it was gender inclusive. Jesus said, *"All that the Father gives me will come to me; and whoever comes to me I will never drive away."* John 6:37 NIV

First at the Cradle, Last at the Cross

Perhaps it is no wonder that a woman was the first at the Cradle and last at the Cross. They had never known a man like this man; there never has been such another. A prophet and teacher who never nagged at them, never flattered them or coaxed or patronized; who never made jokes about them, never treated them as "The women, God help us." or "The ladies, God bless them!" who rebuked and praised without condescension; who took their questions and arguments, seriously; who never mapped out their sphere for them, never urged them to be feminine or jeered at them for being female; who had no axe to grind and no uneasy male dignity to defend; who took them as He found them and was completely unselfconscious. There is no act, no sermon, no parable in the whole Gospel that speaks of female perversity; nobody could possibly guess from the words and deed of Jesus that there was anything "funny" about woman's nature.

As we look at the way Jesus' ministry revolutionized the lives of women: we'll see that what He offered was totally different from their usual treatment in a male-centered world.

For Jesus, there was;

- No double standard
- No exclusion
- No limits on a woman's God-given

Getting ready to go minister.
In front of our home in Broken Arrow, Oklahoma.

Lesson 5

Broke Down the Walls

Jesus Broke Down the Walls for Women

There's a danger when we approach well-known, loved passages of Scripture. The danger is that we will not really hear the words. We have become so used to Jesus' words in the Gospels that we have a hard time not skipping over them. Or we read the familiar words and screen them through our childhood memories, unconsciously coloring them with all the cultural tones in which we grew up.

When it comes to the subject of this course, however, there is no more important time to hear clearly Jesus' words in Scripture. We must imagine their impact on His first audience, who lived in a culture entirely different from ours. When it comes to what was considered "normal" in the ways that males and females related to each other in first-century Israel, Jesus' words and actions were controversial, provocative, even revolutionary.

As I said before, Jesus' mission wasn't gender biased; it was gender inclusive. We're going to look at the way Jesus' ministry revolutionized the lives of women. We'll see that what He offered was totally different from their usual treatment in a male-centered world: No double standard, no exclusion, no limits on their God-given destiny.

- **Mary** *(Luke 1)*

Anna a Prophetess: recognized and proclaimed Him as the Messiah in *(Luke 2:36-38)* The Redemption of Israel.

Luke 2:36-38
36. And there was one Anna, a prophetess, the daughter of Phanuel, of the tribe of Aser: she was of a great age, and had lived with an husband seven years from her virginity;
37. And she was a widow of about fourscore and four years, which departed not from the temple, but served God with fastings and prayers night and day.
38. And she coming in that instant gave thanks likewise unto the Lord, and spake of him to all them that looked for redemption in Jerusalem.

- **Woman caught in adultery?** *(Read: John 8:1-11)*

Why do we call it the story of the woman caught in adultery? Can a woman commit adultery by herself? It's impossible! She couldn't have been "caught in the very act" alone. And what about the biblical law the men were suppose to be so zealously upholding? It stipulated that in the case of adultery, both man and woman were to be put to death.

Leviticus 20:10
And the man that committeth adultery with another man's wife, even he that committeth adultery with his neighbour's wife, the adulterer and the adulteress shall surely be put to death.

(See also: Deut. 22:23)

Why did these "teachers of the law" forget to arrest the other guilty party? Why was he allowed to grab his clothes and scurry away? The truth was their actions were governed more by the double standards of their culture than by the Word of God.

Jesus didn't point that out to them. It was obvious, almost ludicrous. Perhaps a sad smile crossed His lips as He squatted down to write silently in the dust with His finger.

Don't you wonder what He wrote? We aren't told, but we are shown that Jesus refused to be pulled into their biased judgement. Jesus wouldn't support a culture that favored one gender over the other. He refused to approve a double standard. He rebuked the cry of His own and of subsequent ages: "Stone the woman and let the man go free."

Finally He spoke. His words were few, but they stripped His audience bare. *"If anyone of you is without sin, let him be the first to throw a stone at her."* As He bent down again and continued to write His message in the dirt, silence and guilt settled over the mob. Shame replaced anger. One by one they slipped away.

John 8:7-9
7. So when they continued asking him, he lifted up himself, and said unto them, He that is without sin among you, let him first cast a stone at her.
8. And again he stooped down, and wrote on the ground.
9. And they which heard it, being convicted by their own conscience, went out one by one, beginning at the eldest, even unto the last: and Jesus was left alone, and the woman standing in the midst.

Jesus words were few, but they spoke volumes. Sin was sin, whether it was committed by a man or a woman. Every one of us will stand before God in judgement. No one will be able to hide or slip away. No one will be able to point to or blame another.

The woman's sin wasn't worse than the man's, nor was it better. When equity (equality) is the standard, stones are rarely thrown.

Love Between Equals

Matthew 19:3-12
3. The Pharisees also came unto him, tempting him, and saying unto him, Is it lawful for a man to put away his wife

for every cause?
4. And he answered and said unto them, Have ye not read, that he which made them at the beginning made them male and female,
5. And said, For this cause shall a man leave father and mother, and shall cleave to his wife: and they twain shall be one flesh?
6. Wherefore they are no more twain, but one flesh. What therefore God hath joined together, let not man put asunder.
7. They say unto him, Why did Moses then command to give a writing of divorcement, and to put her away?
8. He saith unto them, Moses because of the hardness of your hearts suffered you to put away your wives: but from the beginning it was not so.
9. And I say unto you, Whosoever shall put away his wife, except it be for fornication, and shall marry another, committeth adultery: and whoso marrieth her which is put away doth commit adultery.
10. His disciples say unto him, If the case of the man be so with his wife, it is not good to marry.
11. But he said unto them, All men cannot receive this saying, save they to whom it is given.
12. For there are some eunuchs, which were so born from their mother's womb: and there are some eunuchs, which were made eunuchs of men: and there be eunuchs, which have made themselves eunuchs for the kingdom of heaven's sake. He that is able to receive it, let him receive it.

(See also: Mark 10:2-12)

This wasn't the only time Jesus cut across everyone's beliefs. In fact His teaching on marriage and divorce was downright shocking. Jesus presupposed that women had rights and responsibilities equal to men. Ironically, it was His enemies who gave Him the opportunity to teach on marriage and divorce. The

Pharisees hoped to trap Him by bringing up the controversial subject of divorce. It's very important to listen to Jesus' reply, for it did more than show God's broken heart over divorce. Jesus also directed their eyes back to what everyone had forgotten: The equality of men and women that God established in the Garden of Eden. Jesus referred to *Genesis 1:27 "But at the beginning of creation God made them male and female."* This laid the foundation for the rest of His argument: because men and women had the same origin, they should have equal rights and obligations.

Then He reminded them of the first marriage counselor, God Himself, who advised. *"For this reason a man will leave his father and mother and be united to his wife."* What was Jesus implying as He took them back to Genesis 2? By this time the Jew's idea of marriage and gender roles were distorted and far from God's original plan. Their thinking was more like the nations surrounding them, which were ruled by Greek thought and reinforced by Roman customs. For a young Roman girl, marriage meant a complete break with everything she had known. Even her gods were taken from her when she moved into her husband's family compound.

Jesus' words were radically different. He was saying that the woman wasn't inferior in any way. The man was told to take the initiative in relinquishing rights to his family, in order to enter into marriage with her. It was simply unheard of!

Jesus also highlighted the unity and equality of husbands and wives, quoting further from Genesis

".... and the two will become one flesh." They are still two individuals, but one in love. The Hebrew one is a compound singular word, like a cluster of grapes or a pair of shoes. It's the same word used in the most important proclamation of Judaism: *"Hear, O Israel: The Lord our God, is one Lord." (Deu. 6:4)* So

the unity God intended between a husband and wife is like the unity that God the Father, God the Son, and God the Holy Spirit have enjoyed for eternity. This is part of the significance of that statement, *"Let us make .... in our image .... male and female."* As there is no hierarchy in the Trinity, no inferior or superior in the unity of the Trinity so there cannot be any between a husband and his wife or male and female.

Jesus Did Away With the Double Standard

Then Jesus added a direct command: *"What God has joined together, let not man separate.:"*

Matthew 19:6
Wherefore they are no more twain, but one flesh. What therefore God hath joined together, let not man put asunder.

He was doing more than condemning divorce here. He was also commanding us not to separate people according to human systems of value. We can't have one standard for men and another for women. A double standard is another way of separating what God has joined together.

Even His disciples were amazed when they heard these words. Jesus was holding men and women to the same standard! They sputtered, "If this is the situation between husband and wife, it is better not to marry." Why if men had to play by the same rules as women, they'd have to think twice about marrying. Jesus had leveled the playing field.

What if divorce is inevitable? Jesus said that this tragedy comes as a result of the hardness of our hearts. But even if the unthinkable happens, and there is a divorce, the woman has equal rights and responsibilities with the man. If he divorces his wife and marries or if she divorces her husband and marries, both commit adultery; Equality.

Jesus was coming against hundreds of years of rabbinical teaching, both the right of betrothal and the right of divorce belonged exclusively to men.

Jesus' words didn't weaken marriage. On the contrary, they strengthened it by pointing back to God's initial plan for marriage: a lifelong discovery of love and intimacy between equal partners.

Another story reveals how radically Jesus challenged the rabbis' double standards. In *Luke 13*, Jesus was teaching in the synagogue when He spotted a crippled woman, bent over double. Jesus called her to come forward. When He laid hands on her, she immediately stood up straight, completely healed.

> *Luke 13:10-17*
> *10. And he was teaching in one of the synagogues on the sabbath.*
> *11. And, behold, there was a woman which had a spirit of infirmity eighteen years, and was bowed together, and could in no wise lift up herself.*
> *12. And when Jesus saw her, he called her to him, and said unto her, Woman, thou art loosed from thine infirmity.*
> *13. And he laid his hands on her: and immediately she was made straight, and glorified God.*
> *14. And the ruler of the synagogue answered with indignation, because that Jesus had healed on the sabbath day, and said unto the people, There are six days in which men ought to work: in them therefore come and be healed, and not on the sabbath day.*
> *15. The Lord then answered him, and said, Thou hypocrite, doth not each one of you on the sabbath loose his ox or his ass from the stall, and lead him away to watering?*
> *16. And ought not this woman, being a daughter of Abraham, whom Satan hath bound, lo, these eighteen*

years, be loosed from this bond on the sabbath day?
17. And when he had said these things, all his adversaries were ashamed: and all the people rejoiced for all the glorious things that were done by him.

Just another healing? Hardly. By Jesus' day, women had been completely marginalized in places of worship. Women were relegated to the back of the synagogue, separated from the men. Jesus' invitation to this crippled woman struck out against the male monopoly of public worship. When Jesus put her in the spotlight, right down in front of the whole synagogue, He shattered the men's world view. There must have been a collective gasp from dignified rows of men that day. Didn't Jesus know what He was doing? Women were supposed to be kept in their place, hidden behind the dividing screens.

The leader of the synagogue put words to everyone's disapproval that day. However, he shifted the focus from Jesus' deliberate snubbing of social convention onto safer territory the importance of honoring the Sabbath. What followed next compounded their outrage. Jesus defended Himself by saying "ought not this daughter of Abraham" be loosed, even on the Sabbath?

There was no precedent for Jesus' use of the phrase "daughter of Abraham." Nowhere in rabbinical teaching was an individual woman called "a daughter of Abraham." Jewish men were often referred to as "sons of Abraham." but never women. Everyone knew that women weren't heirs of Abraham in the way men were. But Jesus lavished this term on a woman, and an old use-to-be crippled woman at that.

There was another reason that woman stood straight and tall that day in the synagogue. Jesus had done more than heal her back. He had restored her dignity as a person, showing her that she was valued by God. She was an equal heir with her male counterparts to all God had promised Abraham.

No Exclusion

Jesus didn't exclude women either by word or action. He deliberately chose words that emphasized His common standing with men and women.

Words are important because they show what we believe. So it's important to see the words Jesus used, especially the ones He used about Himself. The most common term He used for Himself was "Son of Man." (31 times in Matthew; 14 times in Mark; 26 times in Luke; and 12 times in John.)

Because of our limitation to our own language, this sounds like He was emphasizing His maleness, but He wasn't. The Greek word '*anthropos*' used in the phrase "Son of Man" is a gender inclusive word. It is better translated as "human" or "person" than it is man. Jesus was affirming the amazing reality of the Incarnation. He was simply saying, "I am human."

We know of course, that Jesus was a male human being. But, the Bible never dwells on His maleness. Jesus was also a Jew, but that wasn't a priority either. The important thing was that He was truly human, fully identified with us in every way.

Hebrews 2:14-18
14. Forasmuch then as the children are partakers of flesh and blood, he also himself likewise took part of the same; that through death he might destroy him that had the power of death, that is, the devil;
15. And deliver them who through fear of death were all their lifetime subject to bondage.
16. For verily he took not on him the nature of angels; but he took on him the seed of Abraham.
17. Wherefore in all things it behoved him to be made

like unto his brethren, that he might be a merciful and faithful high priest in things pertaining to God, to make reconciliation for the sins of the people.
18. For in that he himself hath suffered being tempted, he is able to succour them that are tempted.

...while being totally God at the same time. As God and as a human, He came to lay His life down for every person, not just for Jews and not just for males.

Why Did Jesus Call God "Father"

It might sound normal to us that He called the first person of the Godhead, Father, but it sounded quite foreign to first-century Jewish ears: for such terminology was very rare in the Old Testament.

Why, then, did Jesus call God "Father"? Was He saying God was masculine, like human fathers? No, He was trying to give an image that His listeners could grasp, a term that showed just how intimate God wanted to be with them.

A common Jewish term for God was "the God of Abraham, Isaac, and Jacob." When those words were first used hundreds of years earlier, they sounded intimate and personal. They referred to the God whom those men had met personally. But, as generations passed that reality slipped away. He became the God of long-dead fathers. Tradition replaced personal experience. It became more important to be a descendent of Abraham, Isaac, and Jacob than to know the GOD these men knew.

Jesus shook up everything when He constantly referred to God as "our Father." However, He wasn't saying God was a male. In fact by using "God our Father" instead of "Father God," He was putting distance between His ideas and those of centuries of fertility cults in that part of the world. The ancient religions of the land had always worshiped a "father god" (Baal in earliest times) and his female counterpart, the "mother goddess" (Asherah).

These cults had been absorbed into the popular Gentile religions of Jesus' day. Such ideas of God and His nature had always threatened to seduce the Jews. That's why the Lord specifically commanded them not to make male and female images of God. *(See: Deuteronomy 4:15-16)* He didn't want them, or us, to make the mistake of attributing gender as quality He built into His creatures, Him, the Creator. So, Jesus avoided the cultic "Father God" and called Him, "God our Father."

God was referred to as "Father" nineteen times in the Old Testament, but God was also described in feminine terms in the Hebrew scriptures. One dramatic instance was in Isaiah 42:13-14, where God is likened to a mighty man marching to battle and then to a woman in childbirth.

Isaiah 42:13-14
13. The LORD shall go forth as a mighty man, he shall stir up jealousy like a man of war: he shall cry, yea, roar; he shall prevail against his enemies.
14. I have long time holden my peace; I have been still, and refrained myself: now will I cry like a travailing woman; I will destroy and devour at once.

On at least two occasions Jesus spoke of God using feminine terminology in the parable of a woman searching for a coin and in the parable of a woman hiding yeast in a loaf.

Matthew 13:33
Another parable spake he unto them; The kingdom of heaven is like unto leaven, which a woman took, and hid in three measures of meal, till the whole was leavened.

(See also: Luke 15:8-10; 13:20-21)

He wasn't saying that God was both male and female, nor were others in the Bible who used both masculine and feminine metaphors for the Lord. God is neither male nor female. He is greater than what He has created, including gender distinctions. Indeed, Jesus' words suggest that our human gender distinctions may not be as enduring as we might think.

When asked about the Resurrection, Jesus said we wouldn't marry or be given in marriage in heaven, because we would become "like the angels."

Matthew 22:30
For in the resurrection they neither marry, nor are given in marriage, but are as the angels of God in heaven.

(See also: Mk. 12:25)

His words meant that in eternity, gender distinctions will either be nonexistent or be irrelevant. Therefore, if we are living in light of that eternity, we should not discriminate according to gender now.

A New Initiation Rite

Jesus brought the dawn of a new day. Before ascending into heaven, He gave final instructions to His disciples.

Matthew 28:19-20
19. Go ye therefore, and teach all nations, baptizing them in the name of the Father, and of the Son, and of the Holy Ghost:
20. Teaching them to observe all things whatsoever I have commanded you: and, lo, I am with you alway, even unto the end of the world. Amen.

Mark 16:15-18
15. And he said unto them, Go ye into all the world, and preach the gospel to every creature.

16. He that believeth and is baptized shall be saved; but he that believeth not shall be damned.
17. And these signs shall follow them that believe; In my name shall they cast out devils; they shall speak with new tongues;
18. They shall take up serpents; and if they drink any deadly thing, it shall not hurt them; they shall lay hands on the sick, and they shall recover.

Note: Jesus' disciples baptized believers even during His earthly ministry. *(John 3:22-26, 4:1-2)* He established a sacrament designed to include persons of both genders in the church, the new people of faith. The old sacrament, circumcision, was only for males. But the new initiation rite Jesus gave was baptism: it was an opportunity for both men and women to make a public declaration that they had joined the people of God.

As recorded by the Gospel writers, women were an integral part of Jesus's life and ministry. The record of their presence stands in stark contrast with the literature of the ancient world. Women were nearly silent through the centuries of Jewish literature, the Mishnah and Talmud. But, the Gospels are markedly different, Matthew, Mark, and Luke wrote of women in 112 distinct passages. John makes many extended references to women, such as the Samaritan, and Martha and her sister Mary which we'll look at later.

The most striking thing about the role women played in Jesus' life and teaching is the simple fact they were there, at all. It was nothing short of revolutionary. Jesus saw women as persons He came to reach and serve. He treated them as individuals of worth and dignity, unlike Jewish society, which often viewed women as property.

Charles R. and Mary Ann England in Cookville, Tennessee

Lesson 6

Unlimited Destiny

Women: Jesus put No limits on your God-given Destiny

Not only were women present, as He ministered, they were participating. Jesus taught them the Gospel, the meaning of the Scriptures, and religious truths in general. Most Jews considered it improper, even obscene, to teach women the Scriptures. Jesus's actions were deliberate decisions to break this discrimination against women. (Some have even said Jesus is a Feminist)

Jesus included women when He taught in public. Its interesting that He didn't choose the temple of Jerusalem as His usual place to give public teaching. Instead most of His teaching ministry took place in the towns and countryside around the Sea of Galilee, where no dividing walls segregated women from men. Jesus could teach both men and women. Matthew, writing for a Jewish audience, faithfully records the presence of women at these public teaching sessions. It was something novel and therefore noteworthy.

Matthew 15:38
And they that did eat were four thousand men, beside women and children.

(See also: Matt. 14:21)

Even when Jesus did teach in the temple, He picked the more public areas, the outer courts where women were allowed, so that they also could hear Him speak. *(Ref: John 8:20, 10:23)*

Foundation Stone of Truth Laid by a Woman

Jesus also taught women in private settings. One such incident took place in the home of Mary and Martha, the sisters of Lazarus.

Luke 10:38-42
38. Now it came to pass, as they went, that he entered into a certain village: and a certain woman named Martha received him into her house.
39. And she had a sister called Mary, which also sat at Jesus' feet, and heard his word.
40. But Martha was cumbered about much serving, and came to him, and said, Lord, dost thou not care that my sister hath left me to serve alone? bid her therefore that she help me.
41. And Jesus answered and said unto her, Martha, Martha, thou art careful and troubled about many things:
42. But one thing is needful: and Mary hath chosen that good part, which shall not be taken away from her.

Luke tells us that Mary "sat at the Jesus' feet listening to what He said." To "sit at the feet" of a teacher was a common expression used to show the formal mentoring relationship between a rabbi and his disciple.

Luke 10:39
And she had a sister called Mary, which also sat at Jesus' feet, and heard his word.

Luke is indirectly telling his readers that Mary was taking a position typical of a rabbinic pupil. Its the same expression Paul used to describe his education under Gamaliel. *(Ref: Acts 22:3)* The fact that Luke authored both of these passages assures us that this is an appropriate parallel.

The collection of rabbinical teaching - the Mishnah-exhorted its readers,

"Let thy house be a meeting-house for the Sages and sit amidst the dust of their feet and drink their words with thirst."

In the very next paragraph however, the Mishnah states,

'Talk not much with womankind.....he that talks much with womankind brings evil upon himself and neglects the study of the Law and at the last will inherit hell.'

Though the house was to be a forum for training, women weren't allowed to participate.

Jesus defied the rabbinical exclusion, of women from education. He defended Mary's right to learn as His disciple, saying *"Mary has chosen that good part, which shall not be taken away from her."*

Mary wasn't the only one who benefited from Jesus' private instruction. Jesus also taught Martha at the time of Lazarus' death. "When Martha heard that Jesus was coming, she went out to meet Him." Over the next few verses, Jesus privately engaged Martha in one of the most significant dialogues in the Gospels. The two of them grappled with theological truth in the midst of their shared pain over the loss of Lazarus.

Jesus said to Martha, *"I am the resurrection and the life. He that believeth in me though he were dead, yet shall he live. And whosoever liveth and believeth in me shall never die. Believest thou this?"*

(Read: John 11:17-44)

Jesus didn't give this central tenet of our faith, this intimate self-revelation, to any of the twelve apostles. These words are some of our most treasured in the church. They are often repeated during times of our greatest pain, at deathbeds and funerals. But we might not have these words if Jesus hadn't taken time to teach crucial theological issues to a woman. Nor would we have them if that woman hadn't chosen to pass on her private lesson to the rest of us. It is significant that Luke had more verses (114 Total) with women as the subject than any other Gospels. Luke was Paul's traveling companion and intimate disciple. Had Paul been less sympathetic than Jesus toward women, one would have expected his disciple to avoid their inclusion in his record of the Gospel story. The reverse is true, suggesting to us that Paul's influence on Luke, led Luke to highlight Jesus' inclusion of women.

Jesus didn't just declare truth to Martha. Like any good teacher, He actively engaged her mind, prompting her to think through the implications. He asked, "Do you believe this?" (Also the follow through question in verse 40)

John 11:26-27
26. And whosoever liveth and believeth in me shall never die. Believest thou this?
27. She saith unto him, Yea, Lord: I believe that thou art the Christ, the Son of God, which should come into the world.

Martha's statement in John's account is virtually identical to Peter's confession reported in the other three Gospels.

Matthew 16:16
And Simon Peter answered and said, Thou art the Christ, the Son of the living God.

(See also: Mark 8:29; Luke 9:20)

On that occasion, Jesus replied to Peter by saying he was *'petros'*, meaning "little rock", and upon this *'petra'*, or "big rock," He would build His church. Jesus wasn't saying that Peter was going to be the foundation stone of the church. He was saying that upon, this confession-that Jesus is the Christ, the Son of

God come into the world-His entire church would be built!

The foundation stone of our faith was declared by Martha, as well as Peter. Both understood who Jesus was. Both equally declared truth revealed to them by the Holy Spirit. It we accept this foundational teaching from Peter, a man, we must also accept it from Martha, a woman. If we consider that Peter's spiritual insight was a significant qualification for his spiritual leadership, should we think any differently in the case of Martha?

Three Times an Outcast

Another woman Jesus took time to instruct was the Samaritan woman at the well. *(John 4:6-29)* In fact this is the longest recorded conversation Jesus had with any individual.

John 4:6-29
6. Now Jacob's well was there. Jesus therefore, being wearied with his journey, sat thus on the well: and it was about the sixth hour.
7. There cometh a woman of Samaria to draw water: Jesus saith unto her, Give me to drink.
8. (For his disciples were gone away unto the city to buy meat.)
9. Then saith the woman of Samaria unto him, How is it that thou, being a Jew, askest drink of me, which am a woman of Samaria? for the Jews have no dealings with the Samaritans.
10. Jesus answered and said unto her, If thou knewest the gift of God, and who it is that saith to thee, Give me to drink; thou wouldest have asked of him, and he would have given thee living water.
11. The woman saith unto him, Sir, thou hast nothing to draw with, and the well is deep: from whence then hast thou that living water?
12. Art thou greater than our father Jacob, which gave us the well, and drank thereof himself, and his children, and

his cattle?
13. Jesus answered and said unto her, Whosoever drinketh of this water shall thirst again:
14. But whosoever drinketh of the water that I shall give him shall never thirst; but the water that I shall give him shall be in him a well of water springing up into everlasting life.
15. The woman saith unto him, Sir, give me this water, that I thirst not, neither come hither to draw.
16. Jesus saith unto her, Go, call thy husband, and come hither.
17. The woman answered and said, I have no husband. Jesus said unto her, Thou hast well said, I have no husband:
18. For thou hast had five husbands; and he whom thou now hast is not thy husband: in that saidst thou truly.
19. The woman saith unto him, Sir, I perceive that thou art a prophet.
20. Our fathers worshipped in this mountain; and ye say, that in Jerusalem is the place where men ought to worship.
21. Jesus saith unto her, Woman, believe me, the hour cometh, when ye shall neither in this mountain, nor yet at Jerusalem, worship the Father.
22. Ye worship ye know not what: we know what we worship: for salvation is of the Jews.
23. But the hour cometh, and now is, when the true worshippers shall worship the Father in spirit and in truth: for the Father seeketh such to worship him.
24. God is a Spirit: and they that worship him must worship him in spirit and in truth.
25. The woman saith unto him, I know that Messias cometh, which is called Christ: when he is come, he will tell us all things.
26. Jesus saith unto her, I that speak unto thee am he.
27. And upon this came his disciples, and marvelled that he talked with the woman: yet no man said, What seekest thou? or, Why talkest thou with her?
28. The woman then left her waterpot, and went her way

into the city, and saith to the men,
29. Come, see a man, which told me all things that ever I did: is not this the Christ?

This woman was well acquainted with being an outcast. As a Samaritan, she was rejected by Jews. As a woman, she had been marginalized by men, except when they wanted her sexual services. As an immoral woman, she was even shunned by other Samaritan women. (John records in verse 6, that she came to the well at "about the sixth hour" or about noon, an unusual hour since trips to the well were customarily made in the early morning. Her tardiness was probably due to her nighttime sexual services and her desire to avoid contact with the respectable women who would have chided her for her ways.) She was among the least valued of her day, however Jesus didn't add to her rejection. He looked past her hardened features and gaudy clothing and took her seriously, speaking to her as an equal.

The woman reacted with surprise to Jesus' openness, asking a question in v.9 about the racial tension of the day. Jesus didn't brush her aside. He didn't say "Don't worry your pretty little head about that. Leave those questions to the men folk!" Instead, He gave this "bimbo" an invitation to a serious theological discussion. And, the woman responded, asking a question about her faith. Jesus listened to her. He answered her questions. He spent time with her. He included her. Not only that, He gave her one of the most significant statements about God in the whole of Scripture: *"God is a spirit and His worshipers must worship Him in spirit and in truth." - John 4:24* To her, Jcsus stated for the first time, even before Peter and Martha came to understand this truth, that He was the Messiah.

John 4:25-26
25. The woman saith unto him, I know that Messias cometh, which is called Christ: when he is come, he will tell us all things.

26. Jesus saith unto her, I that speak unto thee am he.

This is the first of the "I AM" statements that form the theological backbone of the Gospel of John.

For Jesus, this encounter with a person outcast in three ways was just as significant as the one He had with Nicodemus, a distinguished Jewish leader. *(Ref: John 3:1-21)* In fact, Jesus spent more time, explaining the ways of God to a woman than to Nicodemus. Jesus directed His full attention to instructing a rejected woman in the ways of God.

What happened when the disciples returned from their grocery shopping and found Jesus immersed in this theological discussion at the well? John said they "marveled that He talked with a woman." It wasn't her race that alarmed them, but her gender. The situation brought out their male-centered view of the world.

Jesus seized this opportunity to enlighten the disciples. In John 4:35, He gave them two commands: (1) lift up your eyes and (2) look. If He had just said, "Look," it might have sounded like a common opening to any declaration. But when He said "Lift up your eyes, and look," He was telling His disciples: "Look at the situation in a new way. Your world view is too small! Take off your cultural blinders that keep you from seeing. I want to stretch your mind. I want you to see people in a new way." That included seeing women in a new way. Women were to be included; they were part of the harvest Jesus had come to reap.

The Samaritan woman rushed off immediately to become an evangelist. She went into the city saying, "Come, see a man who told me everything I ever did. Could this be the Christ?" Her ministry was very successful. Many in her hometown "believed in Him because of the woman's testimony."

The epilogue to this story of "the well side classroom" is given by John, the eyewitness, in verse 42, the woman had led them to Jesus, her converts declared, "Now we believe, not because of thy saying: for we have heard him ourselves, and know that this is indeed the Christ, the Savior of the world." This declaration is one of the climactic moments of John's Gospel account, all because Jesus treated a despised and alienated woman as He would have treated any other person hungry for truth. She became an Evangelist to her hometown and successfully reaped a harvest.

No Limits On God - Given Destiny

Some may see exclusion in the fact that Jesus chose twelve men to be His apostles. This shouldn't give us the idea that Jesus was setting maleness as a requirement for ministry in His church. If we limit leadership to men, we must also limit leadership to people who were Galilean Jews by birth. In fact, our leadership must also speak Aramaic. Further, only eyewitnesses to His ministry for three years can qualify. This standard was applied once and only once. *(Ref: Acts 1:21-26)* Later as the church grew, it discovered that such requirements for leadership were inappropriate and inadequate. It quickly abandoned them for other criteria as the church spread through the nations.

The question remains, though. Did Jesus allow women to minister? Yes. The Gospel evidence is clear. Women ministered both to and with Jesus. The verb '*diakoneo*' is associated with seven women in the Gospel. This is the same verb that describes the ministry of seven men appointed to leadership in the early church. Though the ministry of the seven "deacons" is well known, the ministry of the lesser-known women "deacons" to Jesus and His followers was equally important.

These women were

- Peter's mother-in law

- Mary Magdalene
- Mary the mother of James and Joses
- Salome, the mother of Zebedees sons
- Joanna, the wife of Cuza
- Susanna
- Martha, sister of Mary and Lazarus

These women are held up as examples of those whose servant ministry blessed Jesus and His followers. Same word as males we call deacons in the Book of Acts. Both were servant ministries.

Luke says something interesting in Luke 8:1-3

Luke 8:1-3
1. And it came to pass afterward, that he went throughout every city and village, preaching and shewing the glad tidings of the kingdom of God: and the twelve were with him,
2. And certain women, which had been healed of evil spirits and infirmities, Mary called Magdalene, out of whom went seven devils,
3. And Joanna the wife of Chuza Herod's steward, and Susanna, and many others, which ministered unto him of their substance.

The unique phrase "*the twelve were with Him, and certain women*" makes me wonder: Did these women have a special, publicly recognized role similar to the twelve? No matter what we think, the Gospels tell of women who were constantly part of Jesus' ministerial entourage. Luke speaks of "the women also, which came with Him from Galilee," as a definite and recognized part of His ministerial team.

Luke 23:55
And the women also, which came with him from Galilee, followed after, and beheld the sepulchre, and how his body was laid.

We don't know all they did as they traveled with Jesus. But, come to think of it, we have very little evidence of how the twelve spent their days.

The significant thing is "the women" were regularly with Jesus, just like the twelve. And wasn't this the primary reason Jesus called people to Himself?

Mark 3:14b
... that they should be with him, and that he might send them forth to preach,

We have seen that these women, like the twelve, spent regular time with Jesus. But what of the second part of Jesus call? What about the words *"that he might send them forth to preach and to have power to heal and to cast out devils."* Perhaps women were included in the seventy whom Jesus sent out to preach. It's a distinct possibility, although we can't be positive one way or another.

(Ref: Luke 10:1; l Cor 9:5)

What we can be sure of is that Jesus commissioned a woman to carry the first proclamation of His Resurrection. He commanded Mary Magdalene,

John 20:17
"Go to my brethren, and say unto them, I ascend unto my Father, and your Father; and to my God and your God."

No higher commission to preach the Gospel was ever given. Why then would anyone ask, should women preach? When the Head of the church Himself sent a woman out to preach the Resurrection before the fearful male disciples had yet comprehension of the fact.

Mary Magdalene wasn't the only one. To the women who came to Him, clasped His feet, and worshiped Him on that first Easter morning Jesus said,

> *Matthew 28:10*
> *"Be not afraid; go tell my brethren that they go into Galilee, and there shall they see me."*

How on earth could anyone question whether to trust women to faithfully preach the Good News today when Jesus trusted them with the first proclamation of the Resurrection? Jesus didn't merely give them permission to preach the Gospel; He commanded them to proclaim the Good News.

Let's look again at one more significant encounter Jesus had with a woman in Luke chapter 11.

> *Luke 11:27-28*
> *27. And it came to pass, as he spake these things, a certain woman of the company lifted up her voice, and said unto him, Blessed is the womb that bare thee, and the paps which thou hast sucked.*
> *28. But he said, Yea rather, blessed are they that hear the word of God, and keep it.*

It demonstrates how Jesus challenged the traditional gender roles of that culture. In their place He created a heavenly standard by which all women and all men can discover their God-given destiny. No longer would women only receive God's blessing through their husbands and sons going to the rabbinical academy to study the Mishnah. In Luke 11:28 Jesus was not dishonoring Mary His mother. All His life He loved and cared for her. He was even concerned for her care when He was on the cross.

John 19:25-27
25. Now there stood by the cross of Jesus his mother, and his mother's sister, Mary the wife of Cleophas, and Mary Magdalene.
26. When Jesus therefore saw his mother, and the disciple standing by, whom he loved, he saith unto his mother, Woman, behold thy son!
27. Then saith he to the disciple, Behold thy mother! And from that hour that disciple took her unto his own home.

Jesus was rejecting the system of thought that for centuries had cut women off from active participation in the things of God. Jesus would have no part in religious values that relegated, exempted, excluded, and limited a person's walk with God or her ministry for God. It would be different in His Kingdom. No more would women have to rely on what their men did to receive God's blessing. The new standard was personal obedience to the Word of God.

Instead of making gender an issue we should ask a candidate for ministry: Have you been faithful to the call of God upon your life? Are you hearing the Word of God and obeying it? If the answer is yes?

There is no God-given limit on your destiny.

At the Kunsta Hotel in Nakuru, Kenya

Life and Ministry

A Photo Journal

Teaching at Happy Church - Nakuru, Kenya

In front of Victory Christian School in Tulsa, Oklahoma.

(above) Charles and Mary Ann England on the platform at Happy Church in Nakuru, Kenya.

(below) Welcome to Happy Church!

(above) Hand raised in Victory, ministering at Northside Christian Center, Tulsa, Oklahoma.

(below) Ministering a Word of Knowledge to Aaron Jones at a Mission's Luncheon in Tulsa, Oklahoma 2007.

On our patio in Broken Arrow, Oklahoma.
Headed out to preach The Word.

Preaching The Word of God in Nakuru, Kenya.

(above) Bishop Joseph Kamau and his wife from Happy Church in Nakuru, Kenya

(below) Ministering at Kitonga Gospel Redeemed Church in Nairobi, Kenya

The 'Joy of The Lord' was evident.
Mary Ann always loved sharing God's Word.

God always confirmed His Word through her with Demonstration; Healings, Miracles and Gifts of the Spirit.

An example of a Life poured out for Jesus.

"GLORY TO GOD!"

Lesson 7

Overthrowing Traditions

Paul Turned His World Upside Down

Everywhere Paul went things were shaken up. Some rejoiced as their lives were transformed. Others reacted out of hatred and fear as Paul threatened their standing. Everywhere he went churches were planted and riots erupted. Paul was no maintainer of the status quo: He threatened the world's systems.

This was evident in the words of the Thessalonians who cried out,

> *Acts 17:6*
> *These that have turned the world upside down are come hither also.*

Wherever Paul ministered, the Gospel disrupted centuries of tradition among pagans and Jews.

It was especially dramatic in Ephesus. The Jewish leaders were jealous of Paul, whose preaching was endangering their status among the Jewish enclave of this powerful multi-cultural city. The pagans hated Paul because a good part of their economy was built on the tourist trade of pilgrims to the famous temple of Artemis. Paul's converts were turning away from the worship of Artemis and taking their money with them. The pagans incited a plot against him and he barely escaped with his life.
(Ref: Acts 19:23-47)

Paul had not just angered human opponents, he had also

stirred up a demonic hornet's nest. His preaching had assaulted the devil's stronghold, the Ephesians' intellectual pride entangled with supernatural occult power and the perverse sensuality of the temple rituals. Nothing today compares with Ephesus of old. Imagine a city with intellectual fame, economic power, artistic splendor, spectacle, sex trade and dark occult powers all in one. No wonder Paul barely escaped with his life.

Years later, Paul would not be so fortunate. While worshiping in the temple in Jerusalem, some Ephesian Jews stirred up another riot against Paul. A Roman centurion saved him from a sure lynching and enabled him to have his day in court.

> *Acts 21:27-36*
> *27. And when the seven days were almost ended, the Jews which were of Asia, when they saw him in the temple, stirred up all the people, and laid hands on him,*
> *28. Crying out, Men of Israel, help: This is the man, that teacheth all men every where against the people, and the law, and this place: and further brought Greeks also into the temple, and hath polluted this holy place.*
> *29. (For they had seen before with him in the city Trophimus an Ephesian, whom they supposed that Paul had brought into the temple.)*
> *30. And all the city was moved, and the people ran together: and they took Paul, and drew him out of the temple: and forthwith the doors were shut.*
> *31. And as they went about to kill him, tidings came unto the chief captain of the band, that all Jerusalem was in an uproar.*
> *32. Who immediately took soldiers and centurions, and ran down unto them: and when they saw the chief captain and the soldiers, they left beating of Paul.*
> *33. Then the chief captain came near, and took him, and commanded him to be bound with two chains; and demanded who he was, and what he had done.*

34. And some cried one thing, some another, among the multitude: and when he could not know the certainty for the tumult, he commanded him to be carried into the castle.
35. And when he came upon the stairs, so it was, that he was borne of the soldiers for the violence of the people.
36. For the multitude of the people followed after, crying, Away with him.

When they brought him to trial, the Ephesian Jews claimed that he had defiled the temple in Jerusalem by bringing a Gentile past Herod's dividing walls into the sacred area reserved for Jewish males. This specific charge wasn't true, but Paul was guilty in another way. In fact his real "crime" was even bigger. He wasn't bringing Gentiles past dividing walls. He was declaring to Gentiles, and to slaves and to women that Jesus had torn down the walls. In the twilight of his life, Paul wrote the Ephesian believers from his prison cell:

Ephesians 2:13-16
13. But now in Christ Jesus ye who sometimes were far off are made nigh by the blood of Christ.
14. For he is our peace, who hath made both one, and hath broken down the middle wall of partition between us;
15. Having abolished in his flesh the enmity, even the law of commandments contained in ordinances; for to make in himself of twain one new man, so making peace;
16. And that he might reconcile both unto God in one body by the cross, having slain the enmity thereby:

As we've seen, Herod's walls in the temple were never God's idea. They were the invention of man; an architectural expression of the social barriers erected by man's ungodly traditions.

Have you ever been to a farm and seen an electrical fence? Long after the power is turned off, the animals remain meekly inside the pasture. After a few times of being jolted, they never try to escape again. That's the way it was with the early church. Jesus had already torn down the walls. But now believers had to be taught to walk into their new freedom.

We'll see how Paul did this in the heart of his letter to the Ephesians.

The Most Unlikely Revolutionary

There couldn't have been a less likely person to challenge the status quo than Paul. As Saul of Tarsus, he was born into privilege as a Roman citizen. He also received the best education available to a Jewish youngster. He was the star pupil of an esteemed master, educated at the feet of Gamaliel, one of the most influential rabbis of the first century A.D. Saul was gifted with a razor-sharp mind and was wholly devoted to everything, he had been taught the Torah of Moses as well as the writings of centuries of accumulated wisdom from the great rabbis.

Saul not only was educated according to the best rabbinic tradition, but also was well acquainted with the Greek and Roman ideas of the day. He had impeccable credentials, and was well traveled. If it hadn't been for an unexpected turn of events on the road to Damascus, we might well be reading the thoughts of Rabbi Saul in the Mishnah today. Everything did change, though, on that day when Saul fell to the ground and was blinded by the light. Much of what he had previously been taught had to be radically altered.

When Paul began teaching others, his ideas couldn't have been more different from the teaching he had received from the rabbis. Paul's ideas were new because they were a revelation from God. They were ideas intended to transform every part of people's everyday lives. For instance, an underlying concept throughout the ancient world was that of the "household code."

This concept was seen in Jewish writing such as the Talmud. Everything in ancient society was built upon the household code, which was the basis for law. The household code was defined by three pairs of relationships:

- husband and wife
- father and child
- master and slave

Everyone's role in society was defined by the household code, no one was excluded. For Greeks, Romans, and Jews, the world was strictly a patriarchy. One person; husband/father/master was in complete control over wife, children and slaves. No one questioned what he did in his household. Individual laws and court rulings upheld his privilege. Submission was a one-way street from wife to husband, from child to father, and from slave to master.

Paul took the household code and stood it on its ear, when he wrote to the Ephesians. He commanded mutual submission.... something unheard of before. No longer should men rule like tyrants in their homes. Submission should be a two-way street. Paul said that God's purpose was to bring all things together in unity in Christ.

Ephesians 1:10
That in the dispensation of the fulness of times he might gather together in one all things in Christ, both which are in heaven, and which are on earth; even in him:

He told believers they had the shared tragedy of sin,

Ephesians 2:1-3
1. And you hath he quickened, who were dead in trespasses and sins;
2. Wherein in time past ye walked according to the course

of this world, according to the prince of the power of the air, the spirit that now worketh in the children of disobedience:
3. Among whom also we all had our conversation in times past in the lusts of our flesh, fulfilling the desires of the flesh and of the mind; and were by nature the children of wrath, even as others.

...but now were heirs together.

Ephesians 2:4-10
4. But God, who is rich in mercy, for his great love wherewith he loved us,
5. Even when we were dead in sins, hath quickened us together with Christ, (by grace ye are saved;)
6. And hath raised us up together, and made us sit together in heavenly places in Christ Jesus:
7. That in the ages to come he might shew the exceeding riches of his grace in his kindness toward us through Christ Jesus.
8. For by grace are ye saved through faith; and that not of yourselves: it is the gift of God:
9. Not of works, lest any man should boast.
10. For we are his workmanship, created in Christ Jesus unto good works, which God hath before ordained that we should walk in them.

There was equality at the foot of the Cross. Equality of forgiveness. Equality of hope. Equality of purpose. Believers were ALL being built together into God's future dwelling.

Ephesians 2:22
In whom ye also are builded together for an habitation of God through the Spirit.

Many use Ephesians 5:22 to show something other than equality before Christ. Many modern translations put verse 22 as a separate sentence, saying, "*Wives submit to your husbands, as to the Lord.*" Was Paul singling out women telling them to submit to their husbands?

Lets consider the precise language of Paul's writing. Because Paul was not a sound-bite communicator, if we try to divide his long complex sentences into good sound-bites, we distort his ideas.

Ephesians 5:15-23 is an excellent idea of Paul's transforming ideas. (READ) These verses form only one sentence in the Greek. While translators have made sentences and paragraphs to make it easier to read, they have separated ideas that were meant to be fused together. If you separate these ideas, it appears Paul is saying something opposite to what the original Greek conveys. Verse 22 isn't a separate sentence at all! Its a continuation of a very long one. To put a paragraph break and subtitle is both unfair and incorrect.

Paul's long sentence hinges on the command "Be filled with the Spirit." Some have used speaking in tongues as a sign of being filled with the Spirit. But here Paul gave another measuring stick. Are we living a life characterized by mutual submission? The Holy Spirit doesn't know any other way to live. He has lived throughout eternity in mutual submission with the Father and the Son. If the Holy Spirit is active in our lives, we'll have the same attitude.

Paul was definitely not urging women to submit to men while allowing men to go scot-free, as all other cultures had done. Because of a grammatical feature called an ellipsis, the verb submit doesn't even appear in the original of verse 22. It really says, "*...wives to your own husbands...*" To fill in the blank, the ancient Greek reader knew to go to the previous phrase of the sentence to find the verb submit. Yes, wives were to submit to their husbands, but in the context of the mutual submission of verse 21. Yes, they were to submit to their husbands in the same way that their husbands were to submit to their wives and all were to submit to one another in the Body of Christ.

Unprecedented, Unheard Of, Extraordinary

Paul went on to describe what being filled with the Holy Spirit would mean in our everyday relationships between wife and husband, child and father, and master and slave. We could call Ephesians 5:18-6:9 Paul's new household code. The results of being filled with the Holy Spirit should not just be experienced in church or prayer meetings. They should also be obvious as we relate to one another at home and on the job. That's where the rubber meets the road, isn't it?

Its hard for us to imagine the impact of Paul's teaching on his original audience. Paul took phrases of the household code familiar to them and said something radically fresh something born in the heart of God, revealed in the Garden of Eden, and made possible through the Cross. In the next 328 words in the Greek, Paul spelled out the responsibilities of the traditionally "greater" (husband/father/master) of the household code to the "lesser" (wife/child/slave). This was new, even shocking. No culture's household code had ever made the "greater" responsible to the "lesser" for anything.

It is especially shocking when we consider the specific commands Paul gave the Ephesian believers. Of 8 commands:

- five are directed to the male head of household
- two are directed to children
- one to slaves
- none to wives

Some may point to Ephesians 5:33. Didn't Paul give an imperative to women when he said, "The wife must respect her husband"? No, not in the Greek. In the original, this verb expresses a desire, a wish, or a hope. This phrase is introduced by the Greek word that means "in order that." This is an independent clause, built upon the first half of verse 33. Paul tells the husband to love his wife in order that she may respect him. You cannot command true respect, it must be earned.

Within Paul's description of the Spirit-filled life in Eph 5:22, 6:9.

• He gave 40 words to describe what being filled with the Spirit would look like for the wife responding righteously to her husband. But then he gave 150 words to describe the husband's responsibilities to his wife. This was Unprecedented!

• Paul gave 35 words to children, showing how they were to behave towards their fathers, but gave 16 words of instruction to fathers. Unheard of!

• He gave slaves 59 words to illustrate what being filled with the Spirit meant for them while giving masters 28 words. Extraordinary!

Fathers and masters had ruled without any restraints until this. A man's control of his household was total. In ancient times, the patriarch could even put his children or slaves to death if he chose to. No one had ever placed constraints on fathers. For the first time, *(See: Ephesians 6:4)* the need for a loving nurturing environment for growing children was highlighted.

Paul did not directly confront slavery. Instead he told slaves to work for their masters as though they were working for Christ, then told masters to treat their slaves "in the same way" because they were equal in God's eyes. Clearly his words undermined slavery. He sowed seeds of social change. It would come through repentance and recognition of human equality before God.

What Paul Didn't Say

He didn't say wives were to obey their husbands. This is striking because he did tell children and slaves to obey. He seemed to spotlight this issue by leaving it out.

Notice how Paul told husbands to love their wives. He used two ideas, each of which he repeated, to underline their importance in the strongest way possible:

- Husbands were to love their wives "as Christ loved the church"
- They were to love them "as their own bodies."
- Husbands were to love their wives "as Christ does the church."
- The husband was to love his wife "as he loves himself."

Could anything be further removed from the abusive heavy-handed "machoism" of the ancient world? What he wrote must have left the Ephesian believers with their mouth hanging open.

The High Value of Women

Just think what that meant when Paul told men to love their wives as Christ loved us . Its one thing to love someone as much as you love yourself. But to love someone as much as Christ loved us is setting the highest standard of love possible. When Jesus died for us, He showed what a high value God placed on us. The cross was God's most tangible expression of how much He loves people. Human beings are extremely precious because the Son of God gave His life for each one of us. Therefore women are to be highly valued. God tells husbands that they should love their wives so much that they'd be willing to lay down their lives for them. Could there be any higher value placed on one's wife, or sister, mother or daughter? God puts high value on women and expects men to also.

A Partner Not a Piece of Property

Paul then recalled Genesis 2:24. What was Paul saying by repeating these words to the Ephesians. Was he saying, "You married her now you have to love her?" Paul underscored what Jesus had already said, Paul reminded the men of Ephesus of God's original design for marriage: The man leaves all behind for his wife. They had seen and been taught the exact opposite with Greek and Romans.

Even the Jews failed to hold on to the values laid out for women in Genesis. Right from the beginning, God had clearly established that a woman was to be treated, not as property that a man may take for himself, but as a partner to whom a man must give himself.

Paul said that God was restoring His intent in Jesus who took the initiative in self-renunciation. Coming to earth and giving Himself for the church. This self-sacrificing, rights-relinquishing, first-in-humility kind of love was to characterize a husband's treatment of his wife. Not since Eden had such a high concept of marriage been portrayed. Not since Eden had woman's value been so recognized, her worth so esteemed. Mutuality was to be the hallmark of the Kingdom of God. Where Christ ruled, respect was something each partner in marriage could give each other. Because Jesus came, women could give themselves in submission to their husbands and men could give of themselves to their wives, taking the initiative in self-renunciation. In Christ, the one-way lane had become a two-way road. Jesus, who had come as Eden's hope, had begun to correct Eden's tragedy.

The Radical Equality of the Gospel

Paul closed his household code by stating the underlying principle for these radical new proposals: We are equal before God for...

Ephesians 6:9b
... knowing that your Master also is in heaven; neither is there respect of persons with Him.

That is the underlying principle beneath the mutual submission of Ephesians 5:21.

Ephesians 5:21
Submitting yourselves one to another in the fear of God.

God simply does not put human beings into hierarchies. The reason we can submit to one another is that God sees us all as one. This is a central tenet of the Gospel. Equality isn't based on a humanistic premise; it is rooted in God's impartiality. Because He treats all humans equally, so should we.

Equality before God is a frequent theme of Paul's writing. One of the clearest examples of Paul attacking the hierarchial status quo is Galatians 3.

Galatians 3:28
There is neither Jew nor Greek, there is neither bond nor free, there is neither male nor female: for ye are all one in Christ Jesus.

Why would Paul say this? Notice the three pairs of relationships are not the three pairs of the traditional household code. This grouping was just as familiar to his audience. Here the father/child pair is replaced with Jew/Gentile. What was Paul stirring in the minds of his original audience with the three pairs, Jew/Greek,slave/free&male/female? This was a deliberate choice on

Paul's part. Paul had been a good, strict Pharisee. He was their golden boy well on his way up the rabbi's ladder of success. So, like all devout Jews of his day, he probably recited this prayer as soon as he awoke each morning.

Blessed be He who did not make me a Gentile;

Blessed be He who did not make me a woman;

Blessed be He who did not make me an uneducated man (or a slave).

Because every pious Jew said this prayer the beraka, as soon as he woke up and before he got out of bed, it was the first thing his wife heard as she lay beside him. Put yourself in her position. You lay in bed every morning hearing these cruel words as your husband thanked God he wasn't you! A slave could become free, Gentiles could convert, but you could never stop being a woman.

This prayer shows how far they had strayed from the equality of the sexes God set forth in Genesis. These words clearly show the prideful heart of rabbinic Judaism, where only free Jewish males could fully participate as the people of God.

Other writings backed up this view. "As for an ass, you are under an obligation that it rest; but as for a Gentile (slave), you are under no obligation to ensure that he should rest." Similarly, a woman was valued at two percent of the value of a man when the Talmud stated that "a hundred women are no better than two men."

It seems Paul deliberately chose these three of the traditional morning prayer to declare in Galatians 3:28 that these distinctions no longer existed. In Jesus Christ, Paul declared all distinctions and categories are swept away. All are one. Galatians 3:28 does not say "God loves each of you, but stay in your places;" it says there are no longer places, no longer categories, no longer differences in rights and privileges, codes and values.

If we are preoccupied with maintaining our status, if we're trying to protect our privileges of some hierarchy taught by our culture, we are acting in a non-Christian way. These reactions are the opposite of the Gospel message. Gentiles, slaves, and women are not less valuable to God.

Jesus came into a darkened world of oppression where walls separated people, where the chains of thousands of years bound so many. Jesus tore down the walls and broke the chains. In Christ there are no Jews or Gentiles, no slave or free, no males or females. All are equal at the foot of the Cross.

Jesus became like the least of us to redeem all of us, no one is excluded; no one is left on the outskirts looking through the lattice of a balcony or through the cloth of a veil. Jesus' death challenged all the established cultural views. No more walls are left standing. We are no longer prisoners or perpetrators of discrimination in any form.

Jesus is our one shared hope. His birth as a human reminds us of our shared origins. His death on the Cross forever heals our shared tragedy. His Resurrection restores us to our shared destiny.

We are all called to sit with Christ in heavenly places, to go into all the world filled with the Spirit, to walk out the Gospel in all our relationships, to stand tall because each of us is valuable in the sight of God.

Lesson 8

Proclaiming Good News

Bringing the Gospel to Sin City, A.D. 50

Any serious student of Paul's view of women should concentrate on I Cprinthinas, for Paul devoted more space to gender issues in this Epistle than any other.

We must keep in mind that his words are only half a dialogue. It's like overhearing someone speaking on the phone. We have to recreate what the other person is saying. Paul's Epistles were written in response to communication; oral reports and letters he received from the churches. Since we don't have the other half of the communication to gain better understanding of this letter we mustt find out everything we can about the situation in Corinth. First lets look at the city itself.

Sordidly Rich, Miserably Poor

Corinth straddled a narrow neck of land four miles wide connecting the two main parts of Greece. All traffic from northern Greece to the south had to pass through Corinth. Also to avoid dangerous waters off the southern tip Greece, most sea merchants from the eastern Mediterranean chose to have their goods carried overland through Corinth before continuing their sea passage westward. This made Corinth a major crossroads, wealthy because of her ability to dominate commerce and trade. Corinth became very wealthy, "a kind of market place ... everywhere full of wealth and an abundance of goods."

However, though Corinth was "a town charming indeed to look upon and abounding in luxuries," the "sordidness of the rich" was constrasted with the "misery of the poor."

The city was both a center of the arts and culture filled with beautiful statues, paintings and highly prized craftsmanship, and host to important athletic events. But Corinth became famous for something else: It was so filled with promiscuous activity that the verb karinthiazesthai, "to live like a Corinthian," meant to live a life of sexual immorality.

A Great Army of Harlots

Like many port cities, Corinth became famous for its sex trade. Aphrodite was the Greek goddess of erotic love (known to the Romans as Venus). She was worshipped throughout the Mediterranean world, but especially in Corinth Because of the sity's reputation for immorality, Plato used the term, "a Corinthian girl" to mean a prostitute. One author wrote of Corinth's "great army of harlots," while another, writing at the time of Christ said:

> ["The temple of Aphrodite was so rich that it owned more than 1,000 temple slaves; prostitues, whom both men and women had dedicated to the goddess. And therefore it was also on account of these women that the city was crowded withpeople and grew rich. For instance, the ship captain freely squandered their money, and hence the proverb, "Not for every man is the voyage to Corinth."]

Besides Corinth's "sacred" prostitutes who gave their earnings to the temple, there were thousands more "secular" prostitutes. These were both central to Corinth's economy. They were also an honored part of the city's spiritual life. The Ancients noted:

[It is an ancient custom in Corinth ... whenever the city prays to Aphrodite in matters of grave importance, to invite as many prostitutes as possible to join in their petitions, and these women add their supplication to the goddess and later present at the sacrifices.]

A Smorgasbord of Cults

Though Aphrodite reigned Supreme, other gods and goddesses were also worshiped. Corinth was a veritable smorgasbord of religious cults. Most of the religion's barred women, the exceptions were the mystery cults, which became very important to women. For example in thesecretive cult of Dionysus, women spent several days on the mountain dancing, drinking and engaging in sexual immorality.

[Female worshippers of Dionysus were known as "mad one," it is significant that the term did not apply to men and that it was usually women who were smitten by the god's mania. They boasted of this altered state of consciousness as a gift from Dionysus, who was the god of wine and madness. These women, who seldom saw the world that lay outside their own front door, hailed him as their liberator, Lusios, Biennially his god, given mania "set them free from shuttle and from loom" and drove them to the mountains to dance and rave and celebrate his revels, free from all restraint."]

Before Paul came, the religions open to Gentile women were ones that often celebrated immorality or insanity. This was the corrupt, deceived city at which Paul arrived preaching the righteousness of Jesus Christ, and His death on the Cross.

When Paul came to Corinth about this year A.D. 50, he met

two Jewish exiles from Rome named Aquila and Priscilla. Since the couple were also tent makers, Paul moved in with them to practice his trade while together they began the church.

Acts 18:2-3
2. And found a certain Jew named Aquila, born in Pontus, lately come from Italy, with his wife Priscilla; (because that Claudius had commanded all Jews to depart from Rome:) and came unto them.
3. And because he was of the same craft, he abode with them, and wrought: for by their occupation they were tentmakers.

Paul was also joined by Silas and Timothy: Paul and his team stayed about two years, preaching the Kingdom of God.

Acts 18:5a
And when Silas and Timotheus were come from Macedonia, ...

The church founded by Paul and his team reflected the highs and lows of Corinth society:

- Some of the new believers came from lifestyles of idolatry, immoral behavior, and financial corruption.
- Some were rich, but most were poor.
- Some were educated, but most were not.
- The church had both Jews and Gentiles.
- The church had slaves and free.
- The church included men and women

This group of people crossed all demographic lines, probably showing far greater diversity than any church you or I have ever attended. This is important to understand when we look at Paul's admonitions to the people.

Priscilla, Paul's Esteemed Colleague

Paul didn't work in isolation. He usually worked with a team, relying on his coworkers to help him proclaim the Gospel and plant the churches. We've already seen that a married couple; Priscilla and Aquila, were on his team in Corinth. These two colleagues also helped plant the church in Ephesus and Rome. Paul expressed great confidence in their leadership skills and considered them among his most trusted coworkers.

Sometimes God calls men to be ministry leaders. Other times, He calls women. And sometimes He calls a couple to serve together. Priscilla and Aquila are an example of this. In the seven times these two are mentioned in the New testament, they are always mentioned together, inseparably linked in ministry. Not only that, but of those seven references, in five of them Priscilla's name comes first. This was contrary to the Roman custom of naming the man first when referring to a couple. In fact, that was so rarely done that it seems to indicate that Priscilla was the more prominent member of this ministry couple.

Acts 18:18-19, 24-26
18. And Paul after this tarried there yet a good while, and then took his leave of the brethren, and sailed thence into Syria, and with him Priscilla and Aquila; having shorn his head in Cenchrea: for he had a vow.
19. And he came to Ephesus, and left them there: but he himself entered into the synagogue, and reasoned with the Jews.

24. And a certain Jew named Apollos, born at Alexandria, an eloquent man, and mighty in the scriptures, came to Ephesus.
25. This man was instructed in the way of the Lord; and being fervent in the spirit, he spake and taught diligently the things of the Lord, knowing only the baptism of John.

26. And he began to speak boldly in the synagogue: whom when Aquila and Priscilla had heard, they took him unto them, and expounded unto him the way of God more perfectly.

(See also: Ro. 16:3-5; I Cor. 16:19; II Tim. 4:19)

So when Acts 18:26 says that together Priscilla and Aquila "invited Apollos to their home and expounded unto him the way of God more perfectly" Priscilla probably took the lead in teaching Apollos the Gospel. Priscilla's pupil went on to have a prominent public ministry. Apollos was apowerfully anointed preacher in Corinth and elsewhere.

Acts 18:27-19:1
27. And when he was disposed to pass into Achaia, the brethren wrote, exhorting the disciples to receive him: who, when he was come, helped them much which had believed through grace:
28. For he mightily convinced the Jews, and that publickly, shewing by the scriptures that Jesus was Christ.
1. And it came to pass, that, while Apollos was at Corinth, Paul having passed through the upper coasts came to Ephesus: and finding certain disciples,

(See also: I Cor. 3:1-4:13, 16:12)

This understanding of Priscilla's contribution was given by John Chrysostom, a church father writing in the fourth century A. D.

[This is worthy of inquiry, why, as he addressed them, Paul has placed Priscilla before her husband. For he did not say, "Greet Aqila and Priscilla," but "Priscilla and Aquila." He does not do this without reason, but he seems to acknowledge a greater godliness for her than for her husband. What I said is not guess work, because it is possible to learn this from the Book of Acts. Priscilla took Apollos, an eloquent man and powerful in the Scriptures, but knowing only the baptism of John; and she instructed him in the way of the Lord and made him a teacher brought to completion.]

These words by John Chrysostom are all the more remarkable because he was known for making many statements against women.

Nothing Unusual

What seemed so obvious to Chrysostom in the fourth century is not clear at all to some Bible teachers today who argue that the word expound or explain *(ektitheimi)* in Acts 18:26 is entirely different from teach *(didasko)* in I Timothy 2:12 where Paul seems to prohibit women from having the same ministry Priscilla had.

Acts 18:26
And he began to speak boldly in the synagogue: whom when Aquila and Priscilla had heard, they took him unto them, and expounded unto him the way of God more perfectly.

I Timothy 2:12
But I suffer not a woman to teach, nor to usurp authority over the man, but to be in silence.

The only reason for splitting semantic hairs is if you start with a bias against women teaching, then try to support that position while excusing obvious Bible examples that contradict it.

No, Luke clearly said that Priscilla with her husband's help, taught Apollos the ways of God. What's astounding is the very natural, almost casual way Luke mentions this. (If Paul actually did teach against women ministers, how can we account for his close companion and colleague reporting Priscilla's contribution in such a matter of fact way? For Luke, there was nothing unusual about the fact that Priscilla was teaching.)

Another writer said,

["One must not overlook that Apollos accepted Priscilla's instruction without reservation. Moreover, neither Luke nor Paul criticize her for having taught a man. If Priscilla had violated Paul's alleged prohibition against the teaching ministry of women it seems likely that either Luke or Paul would have criticized her for having taught a man."]

Other Women Leaders in Corinth

Other women were significant in the life of the Corinthian church. Chloe was mentioned in I Corinthians 1.

I Corinthians 1:11
For it hath been declared unto me of you, my brethren, by them which are of the house of Chloe, that there are contentions among you.

The word 'household' does not appear in the Greek. The Greel literally says "those of Chloe." This phrase grammatically parallels two phrases in Romans 16:10-11. *"Greet those of Aristobulus" "Greet those of Narcissus who are in the Lord"* Paul left out household, in the Greek. It was understood, but not stated in the Greek.

These two greetings are commonly understood to be greetings to home churches led by Aristobulus and Narcissus. How interesting that Paul used the exact same phrase to describe the household of Chloe. It seems Chloe was more than a homeowner; she was a leader of one of the Corinthian house churches.

If Chloe was a leader in the Corinthian church, Paul's words in I Corinthians 1:11 take on new urgency. Paul wasn't responding to some idle gossip that somehow made its way to him. He was responding to the report of an official delegation sent by one of the church's leaders. Paul took Chloe's report seriously.

Paul considered Chloe's evaluation to be trustworthy. Because he believed her assessment of the condition of God's people, we have the book of I Corinthians. If the words of a woman leader in the church of Corinth led to Paul's writing this Epistle, how can we believe that Paul would categorically silence women in the church.

Submitting, Laboring Together

Stephana is mentioned in I Corinthians 16:15-18. Stephana was a woman's name. Since Stephana in this instance was clearly someone in authority, commentators and translators have assumed Stephana was a man, even though the most natural sense of the Greek would seem to point to a woman. Apparantly translators have assumed this because Paul urged the corinthians to submit to Stephana's authority. Could paul ask 'brothers' to submit toa person in leadership if that person was a woman?

I Corinthians 16:15-18
15. I beseech you, brethren, (ye know the house of Stephanas, that it is the firstfruits of Achaia, and that they have addicted themselves to the ministry of the saints,)
16. That ye submit yourselves unto such, and to every one that helpeth with us, and laboureth.

17. I am glad of the coming of Stephanas and Fortunatus and Achaicus: for that which was lacking on your part they have supplied.
18. For they have refreshed my spirit and yours: therefore acknowledge ye them that are such.

If you view submission in a hierarchial way, with the "lesser" individuals submitting to those who are "greater," and if you believe that women are lesser than men, then Paul's words in verses 15 and 16 could pose a real problem. On the other hand, if you understand the mutual submission commanded of all believers, and if you believe in the equality of men and women, there is no problem at all. Something to one another in the Body of christ is a normal part of life in the Spirit.

It doesn't matter if Stephana was a man or a woman. What is important is that Paul urged everyone to submit, help, and to labor at it. These latter two words are forms of Greek words Paul used to describe women whom he considered his peers and partners in ministry:

- *'sunergos'* or coworkers; Euodia, Syntache, and Priscilla *(Ref: Php. 4:1-3; Ro. 16:3, 6, 9)*
- *'kopiao'* or laborer; Mary, Persis, Tryphena and tryphos *(Ref: Ro. 16:12)*

Of the thirty-nine people Paul mentioned as colleagues in ministry, he spoke of the ten women and the twenty-nine men in identical ways.

F. F. Bruce states,

["Paul seems to make no distinction between men and women among his fellow workers. Men receive praise, and women receive praise for the collaboration with him in the Gospel Ministry, without any suggestion that there was any even subtle distinction between the one and the other in respect of status or function."]

VIP Treatment For A Very Important Woman

Last but certainly not least was Phoebe, also associated with the church at Corinth. Paul's words about her in the closing lines of his letter to the Romans tells us much about the status of women in the Corinthian church.

Romans 16:1-2
1. I commend unto you Phebe our sister, which is a servant of the church which is at Cenchrea:
2. That ye receive her in the Lord, as becometh saints, and that ye assist her in whatsoever business she hath need of you: for she hath been a succourer of many, and of myself also.

Evidently, Paul entrusted Phoebe with the important job of carrying his letter to the Roman believers. Let's look carefully at his words to see how he expected the Roman church to receive her.

Paul started off by saying he "commended" Phoebe. The Greek word for 'commend' literally means "to stand with." Paul was saying that he would stand with Phoebe and unreservedly endorsed her. Given the Corinthian context, this commendation was extremely significant.

The Corinthians were obsessed with status. Paul wouldn't play their prideful games. He rebuked those "who commend themselves." It's not he who commends himself but who the Lord commends. Paul wouldn't seek letters of rcommendation for himself that were so coveted by those who aspired to spiritual leadership in the church.

II Corinthians 3:1
Do we begin again to commend ourselves? or need we, as some others, epistles of commendation to you, or letters of commendation from you?

This makes it all the more important that Paul wholeheartedly commended Phoebe. Paul said the Corinthian believers should have commended him and didn't.

II Corinthians 12:11
I am become a fool in glorying; ye have compelled me: for I ought to have been commended of you: for in nothing am I behind the very chiefest apostles, though I be nothing.

He wanted to make sure this didn't happen to Phoebe. So he stood with her, giving her the commendation she merited. In the status-conscious Corinthian church, this was a clear sign of recognized spiritual authority.

No Gender Distinction

After declaring his endorsement of her, Paul used two key words to describe Phoebe. He called her a sister in the same way he often called his male coworkers, brothers. Then he called her a '*diakonos*.' Many translations render this "servant." This is not incorrect, although it might be better to translate it "deacon" or "minister" as is done in other New Testament passages.

However you translate it, the important thing to note is that Paul used the same word here that he often used for his male coworkers. There was no gender distinction in this term for ministers of the Gospel. Both men and women were simply called deacons.

Over the years the church has come to define deacon as something different from full-time minister. In most Protestant churches a deacon is a layperson serving on a board with others, helping the pastor run the business of the local church. However, no such distinction between minister and deacon existed in the New Testament.

This is the only place in the New Testament that the noun *'diskonos'* is modified by the phrase "of the church." Paul wanted his readers to understand that Phoebe wasn't just a servant girl. She was a minister of the Gospel who served the church in a publicly recognizable way.

Then Paul got to the point. Because Phoebe was who Paul said she was, the Romans were supposed to "receive her."

Interestingly Paul tells the Romans to receive her in a way "that becometh saints." Or in a way worthy of saints. Sounds similar to his teaching in I Timothy.

> *I Timothy 5:17*
> *Let the elders that rule well be counted worthy of double honour, especially they who labour in the word and doctrine.*

This shows how strongly Paul was commending Phoebe: He asked his readers to receive her with the same attitude universally due godly church leaders.

Give Her A Blank Check

Paul told the Roman believers to help Phoebe. The word is related to the verb 'commend' meaning literally "to stand with." Just as he stood with Phoebe, Paul wanted them to stand with Phoebe. Plus, he asked them to give her the equivalent of a blank check, saying they were to stand with her in "whatever she may need."

At this point the Roman church might have been wondering, "Just who is this Phoebe anyway, for Paul to ask all this?" Paul told them why she deserved such special treatment, saying she was a '*prostatis*.' The Greek word is rich in meaning, but it appears only this one time in the New Testament. Most translators have used 'helper' here. KJV has 'succourer.' That is far weaker sounding than the word in Greek. 'Servant leader' comes a little closer because it describes a leader who champions the cause of others rather than pursuing self-interest. We don't have a strong enough equivalent in our language. (Yet there is no word in Greek to better describe the godly leadership modeled by Jesus, who said that anyone aspiring to leadership must be servant of all.)

In other ancient literature, *prostatis* was used to describe the noblest, most beneficial rulers. Only one person was so described in the New Testament; Phoebe. Paul couldn't have honored her more.

Paul went on to say "many had benefited from Phoebe's role as servant leader." Her authority had served a great number of people. This was no insignificant role she fulfilled.

Thus we see that the idea of women in ministry leadership was anything but foreign to the Corinthian believers. Capable women had closely collaborated with paul in his mission and endeavors in Corinth. Phoebe, Priscilla, Chloe, and Stephana were significant to the life and leadership of the church in Corinth. This lay in stark contrast to the role of women in other religions of Corinth, whose women either were not allowed at all or participated as objects of lust or as drunken mad-women.

Paul confronted the philosophies of Greeks and Romans and Jews in his teaching on gender roles and showed how men and women were to relate to each other in light of the Cross and its transforming influence. To the Corinthians Paul showed women as persons who were to be fully included as equals in the Body of Christ.

Some say Mary Ann flowed in the same anointing of Kathryn Kuhlman; to meet the needs of those being ministered to.

Cesson 9

A Question of Headship

1 Corinthians 11:2-16

2. Now I praise you, brethren, that ye remember me in all things, and keep the ordinances, as I delivered them to you.

3. But I would have you know, that the head of every man is Christ; and the head of the woman is the man; and the head of Christ is God.

4. Every man praying or prophesying, having his head covered, dishonoureth his head.

5. But every woman that prayeth or prophesieth with her head uncovered dishonoureth her head: for that is even all one as if she were shaven.

6. For if the woman be not covered, let her also be shorn: but if it be a shame for a woman to be shorn or shaven, let her be covered.

7. For a man indeed ought not to cover his head, forasmuch as he is the image and glory of God: but the woman is the glory of the man.

8. For the man is not of the woman; but the woman of the man.

9. Neither was the man created for the woman; but the woman for the man.

10. For this cause ought the woman to have power on her head because of the angels.

11. Nevertheless neither is the man without the woman, neither the woman without the man, in the Lord.

12. For as the woman is of the man, even so is the man also by the woman; but all things of God.

13. Judge in yourselves: is it comely that a woman pray unto God uncovered?
14. Doth not even nature itself teach you, that, if a man have long hair, it is a shame unto him?
15. But if a woman have long hair, it is a glory to her: for her hair is given her for a covering.
16. But if any man seem to be contentious, we have no such custom, neither the churches of God.

We have seen how committed Paul was to the equal standing of every man and woman before God and each other. With this firm foundation under our feet we'll turn to Paul's more difficult passages concerning women.

People who love Jesus want to be obedient to his call upon their lives. The hearts of both men and women who follow Jesus stir with the desire to use their God-given gifts and talents to see the Kingdom of God extended and the Great Commission fulfilled. However three statements of Paul's pose a problem for women committed to obeying the Word of God, and yet feel called to public ministry.

▶ **1.** *I Corinthians 11:3*
But I would have you know, that the head of every man is Christ; and ***the head of the woman is the man;*** *and the head of Christ is God.*

▶ **2.** *l Corinthians 14:34*
Let your women keep silence in the churches: *for it is not permitted unto them to speak; but they are commanded to be under obedience, as also saith the law.*

▶ **3.** *l Timothy 2:12*
But ***I suffer not a woman to teach,*** *nor to usurp authority over the man, but to be in silence.*

So, how can a woman look at these passages and be both faithful to the Word of God and faithful to the gifts and callings God has given her?

Many look at these passages, such as 1 Corinthian 11, and wonder. It appears that Paul is contradicting the equality he has been promoting. What happened to the great equalitarian we saw overturning patriarchal societies, flying in the face of the second-class status given women? Is he backing down or retreating from his previous statements? Is Paul contradicting himself? Does the Bible contradict itself?

Though some passages may at first appear contradictory, we can be sure that God does not contradict Himself. So, lets ask Him for wisdom. There are answers and God always helps us find them if we ask.

James 1:5
If any of you lack wisdom, let him ask of God, that giveth to all men liberally, and upbraideth not; and it shall be given him.

We need to look at any troubling verse in the context to discern its true meaning. So, lets look at the big picture of this section of 1 Corinthians. Starting with 1 Corinthians 11:2, Paul addressed pressing concerns in the corporate life of the Corinthian church. In the following four chapters, he dealt with:

- 1 Corinthians 11:2-6 gender issues in public ministry.
- 1 Corinthians 11:17-34 instructions about the Lord's Supper
- 1 Corinthians 12:1-11 the diversity of God's gifts
- 1 Corinthians 12:12-31a unity in the Body of Christ
- 1 Corinthians 12:31b-13:13 love as the motive for ministry
- 1 Corinthians 14:1-25 the gifts of prophecy and tongues

- l Corinthians 14:26-40 how corporate worship should take place

Leading with Gender Issues

Paul began with gender issues because, evidently, it was one of the leading issues in Corinth. Earlier in this Epistle, he had given teaching that placed men and women as equals and showed each individual's value. Now Paul has turned to how men and women should relate in public ministry.

In l Corinthians 11:2-16, Paul used a method of teaching common in the Bible called "interchange". He alternated between two sets of ideas, different, but related. On one hand, Paul discussed right attitudes; bedrock principles that guide all behavior for all believers every where. On the other hand, he showed the practical outworking of those attitudes in right attire for their society, for first century Corinth. ("A" verse 3)("B" verses 4-7)("A" verses 8-12)("B" verses 13-15) Then he ends with verse 16. This is called the A-B-A-B structure.

"What Did He Mean by Head?"

Read l Corinthians 11:3 Carefully

I Corinthians 11:3
But I would have you know, that the head of every man is Christ; and the head of the woman is the man; and the head of Christ is God.

Was Paul contradicting the equality he had already promoted? Much hinges on the interpretation of the word head.

What comes to mind when you hear head? Probably something like boss, leader, authority, ruler, top dog, the big cheese, or head honcho. Right? It doesn't matter what we think. What matters is what Paul's original readers thought. What image did the word "head" bring to the mind of lst Century Corinthians?

In Greek, the word is '*kephale*'. Like its English equivalent, it is used to refer to the part of the body that sits above our shoulders and it is also used in several metaphorical meanings. When it comes to those meanings, we come to a real battleground between Greek experts. Some believe it could mean "authority over" as it does in English when we say "the head of a department." Others think this Greek word was primarily used to convey the idea of "source" or "origin," as it does in English when we speak of the headwaters of a river. Liddell and Scott list 48 English meanings for *kephale* in their dictionary, and not one of them means "leader," "authority," "first," or "supreme". On the other hand, Bauer's lexicon gives "superior rank" as one of its meanings. How could experts disagree over the meaning of a word?

Several reasons exist for disagreement between the experts. For one, any language is a living thing. Meanings for words change dramatically over time.

Consider the word "gay" and what it meant to our grandparents versus what it means to us today. To our grandparents, gay meant "happy" or "carefree." It was first used to mean "homosexual" in the late 1960s. That happened in a few years, but scholars of ancient Greek are attempting to define words that evolved over many centuries. Imagine how hard to pinpoint the precise meaning of a word during a limited period of time, such as the few decades of Paul's ministry.

Add to that the differences within a language as it is spoken in various parts of the world. Americans discover this when we visit England. If you ask a waiter for another "napkin," you don't realize you've just asked them for a "diaper." Such differences existed in Paul's day too, as educated people from every part of the Roman Empire spoke the Greek language.

Let's discover what the word *kephale* meant to Paul when he said "the kephale of the woman is the man." We'll look at several sources to aid us. For one, we need to look at the ancient Greek translation of Hebrew Scriptures, called the Septuagint. This would have been what Paul used when ministering among Greek speaking people.

The word for "head" in Hebrew is *ro'sh*. It can mean part of a body or "leader" or "ruler." When it meant a physical head in the O.T. the Septuagint translators chose '*kephale*' (the word Paul used in l Corinthians 11:3) to translate it 226 out of 239 times, or 95% of the time. However, when *ro'sh* meant "ruler" or "leader," the Septuagint translators used some other word 171 out of 180 times. They used *kephale* for "ruler" or "leader" only 5% of the time.

It is possible that Paul used *kephale* in l Corinthians 11:3 to mean that man should be the "leader" or "ruler" over woman, but that would be a rare usage of the word, as seen by the evidence of the Septuagint. On the other hand, many many times in ancient literature, head/*kephale* meant "source" or "origin." This came from the ancients' idea that semen, the source of life, was produced in the male brain, which is of course, located in the head. Aristotle believed this and influenced generations after him. Therefore, for Paul's readers, head represented the source of life for them.

Kephale was also the word used for the source of a river. The Greeks and Romans often set up the bearded head of a man or a bull at a fountain or at the source of a river. Still today, in English, we still refer to the source of a river as its headwaters.

So, Which Is It?

If *kephale* could be either "ruler" or "life source," how was Paul using it here? Using each, of those meanings, we come up with two alternatives. (Read l Corinthians 11:3 with each possibility 1. Authority/leader and 2. Source/origin) Which meaning best fits the context of l Corinthians 11? Four things about this passage give us clues.

- **Clue # 1 What's missing?**

If Paul was talking about man being the authority/leader over woman, teaching that women should submit to men's "God-given" leadership, the theme would be woven throughout these verses. But, two things are striking about this passage, because of their absence:

► **1.** The word submission is never used once in the passage.
► **2.** Authority appears only once, and there it speaks of "the authority a woman has over her own head."

What about the other meaning for head/*kephale* as "source/origin"? The idea of origins is found throughout the passage. First of all, the language of verse 7 is reminiscent of the Genesis account. Then verses 8 and 9 talk about how the first woman originated from man. Next, verse 12 brings the idea full circle to say that since then every man has originated from a woman. Paul sums it all up by saying that all originated from God. It is all about origins. If you translate *kephale* as "source/origins," it's a perfect flow within the flow of the passage. But if you try to fit "authority/leader" in verse 3, it doesn't fit the rest of the passage.

• Clue #2 Who Is "The Man"?

Look again at verse 3. See the first two pairs of relationship (every man/Christ, and a woman/the man). The first pair is a universal statement; every man .... Christ. The second pair is specific; about a woman ... the man. Why does Paul shift from the universal to the specific? Who is this "woman," and who is "the man"?

If Paul is talking about husbands being the authority over their wives, why does he switch from "every man" to the singular specific "the man"? Or, since marriage isn't specifically mentioned, is Paul saying any man is the authority over any woman? Or, if this is about marriage, though not mentioned, where would this leave single women? What about widows? Does a mother need to submit to her son?

If you translate head/*kephale* in verse 3 as "authority/leader," you inherit some very messy questions. Also, is Jesus Christ presently the authority/leader of every man on earth? Look around you. Read the headlines. Check out what's on T.V. No, Jesus is not the authority/leader of every person, not yet. Someday every knee will bow, etc. ... but its not that way right now.

On the other hand if we look at l Corinthians 11:3 with head/*kephale* meaning "origin/source," everything falls into place in the entire passage. Jesus is the "source/origin" of everyone and everything, even though not everyone yet acknowledges him as his or her "authority/leader."

Read the following Acts 17:25-28 and l Corinthians 8:6

Acts 17:25-28
25. Neither is worshipped with men's hands, as though he

needed any thing, seeing he giveth to all life, and breath, and all things;
26. And hath made of one blood all nations of men for to dwell on all the face of the earth, and hath determined the times before appointed, and the bounds of their habitation;
27. That they should seek the Lord, if haply they might feel after him, and find him, though he be not far from every one of us:
28. For in him we live, and move, and have our being; as certain also of your own poets have said, For we are also his offspring.

I Corinthians 8:6
But to us there is but one God, the Father, of whom are all things, and we in him; and one Lord Jesus Christ, by whom are all things, and we by him.

Paul spoke this to pagan philosophers in Athens. Translating head/*kephale* as "origin/source" also answers the question Who is "the man" in l Corinthians 11:3? Who else could that man be, but Adam? Adam was the "origin/source for Eve. Once again, Paul was denying the teaching of the Greeks, who claimed that women had a separate and inferior origin. No, Paul said, woman came from man making her fully human and fully equal to man. Paul explains in verses 8 and 9 what he meant in verse 3, when he wrote "*For the man is not of the woman; but the woman of the man.* (Came from) *Neither was the man created for the woman; but the woman for the man.*"

- **Clue # 3 A Question of Who Came First**

Another indication of what Paul meant can be found in the order in which he listed the three pairs: "every man/Christ," "a woman/the man," and "Christ/God." If Paul were giving us a divinely established hierarchy you'd expect him to begin at the top and work his way down.

However, Paul did not list the pairs in a normal flowchart. Instead he began with "every man/Christ, the "a woman/the man," and finally "Christ/God." If Paul meant head/*kephale* to be "authority/leader," he was arranging this supposed hierarchy in a strange order, starting with the second pair, then moving to the third and then jumping back to the first pair. Paul was a very orderly writer. This haphazard listing would be very odd unless he had something entirely different in mind.

If you read "origin/source" instead of "authority/leader" for *kephale*, Paul's list in 1 Corinthians 11:3 make perfect sense. In the order of creation, Adam was created first, from whom "every man"descended. Then God created Eve, "a woman from the man."

Galatians 4:4
But when the fulness of the time was come, God sent forth his Son, made of a woman, made under the law,

Of course, the only begotten Son existed throughout eternity with the Father. In space and time however. "The Word became flesh and dwelt among us" *(See below: John 1:1 and 14)* many generations after Adam and Eve thus following then chronologically.

John 1:1, 14
1. In the beginning was the Word, and the Word was with God, and the Word was God.

14. And the Word was made flesh, and dwelt among us, (and we beheld his glory, the glory as of the only begotten of the Father,) full of grace and truth.

Paul didn't give a hierarchy or flowchart in 1 Corinthians

11:3. He gave a time line.

By now we see that its highly unlikely that Paul meant to convey that man was the "authority/leader" over woman. It simply doesn't fit. However if he meant "source/origin," there's an harmonious flow.

The church fathers agreed with this interpretation. One was Cyril of Alexandria in fifth century A.D.

Its important to see that the only other time Christ was spoken of as "head" in context of gender issues was in Paul's Ephesians "household code." Paul said in *Ephesians 5:23 "For the husband is the head of the wife, even as Christ is the head of the church: and He is the savior."*

If authority had been on Paul's mind, you'd expect him to use "Lord." But, he chose savior. By not using Lord, he deliberately steered away from the concept of authority. Instead he portrayed Him as "Savior," the one who redeemed us from death and is the source of new life. Once again, when Paul discussed gender issues he showed the concept of head/*kephale* as "source/origin" of life.

- **Clue # 4 Christ is Equal to God the Father**

The fourth reason I believe head/*kephale* here should be understood as "source/origin" rather than "authority/leader" is based on the theological implications for the third pair, Christ/God. Jesus voluntarily yielded to His Father's will throughout his earthly ministry. But this doesn't mean that within the Trinity the Son in some sort of permanent one-sided submission to the Father. In fact the mutual submission we're supposed to have in the Body of Christ, flows out of the mutual submission of the Trinity to one another.

The Bible shows us each member of the Trinity lovingly bestowing honor on the others. The Father always commends the Son and works through the Spirit, the Son always yields to the Father and promotes the Spirit and the Spirit always points to the Son and does what the Father says. The Trinity is the ultimate model of servanthood, preferring one another in love and honor, always submitting to one another in perfect unity.

The phrase "the head of Christ is God" cannot mean that there is inequality between the Son and the Father. Jesus is "very God, of very God," fully equal to the Father in every respect. There is no hierarchy in the Trinity. A fourth century church father Athanasius said regarding l Corinthians 11:3 that "head" must be understood as "origin/source" rather than "authority/leader" lest one arrive at a faulty understanding of the Trinity.

Saying Paul meant *kephale* as "authority/leader" gives a distorted image of the Trinity. However, using "source/origin" to interpret *kephale* here, is a straightforward affirmation of the incarnation of Christ. It was sacrificial love that led the Father to allow His Son to leave heaven, to be born on earth, and to give His life to redeem us.

We Need Each Other

l Corinthians 11:8-12
8. For the man is not of the woman; but the woman of the man.
9. Neither was the man created for the woman; but the woman for the man.
10. For this cause ought the woman to have power on her head because of the angels.
11. Nevertheless neither is the man without the woman, neither the woman without the man, in the Lord.

12. For as the woman is of the man, even so is the man also by the woman; but all things of God.

Paul used the Genesis account of creation to remind men and women of shared origins. In verses 8 and 9, he emphasized that both men and women should live in interdependence, leaving no room for either sex to despise the other. Women can't be independent from men because woman was created from man. But, neither can men adopt an attitude of prideful disdain for women, since woman was created because of man's need of her.

Those who see in verse 8 a foundation for male-only leadership, because the male was created first, have regrettably missed the point. As a matter of fact, if chronological sequence qualified or disqualified anyone for ministry or a particular level of leadership, Paul, to whom Christ appeared "last of all," shouldn't have ministered as he did.

Paul was reminding men that Adam was in need of an *'ezer k'neged*, a strong equal partner. God designed Eve for full partnership with Adam, because Adam couldn't do the job without her. He showed male believers in Corinth their need for women to be ministering alongside them, because God designed men and women to work together in interdependence.

Words Not In The Original

Because women are full and equal partners, in ministry, Paul said *"For this reason ... the woman ought to have authority over her own head."* The NIV of this is unacceptable. It adds the phrase "sign of," which does not appear in the original Greek. The phrase "authority over" is *exousia epi*. The word *'exousia'* means "the right, authority, freedom, and decision-making ability."

Paul was simply saying women have the right to wear whatever they want to on their heads, just as men do. Of course, in the context of the rest of Paul's words in l Corinthians, women and men must be guided by love. Right attitudes of heart will dictate what styles will best serve the purposes of the Gospel.

l Corinthians 14:31-33
31. For ye may all prophesy one by one, that all may learn, and all may be comforted.
32. And the spirits of the prophets are subject to the prophets.
33. For God is not the author of confusion, but of peace, as in all churches of the saints.

Paul Adds Some Curious Words

"Because of the angels, the woman should have authority over what she wears on her head." "If because of the angels," is looked up in a dozen commentaries you get a dozen different suggestions as to its meaning. That is because no one knows for sure what Paul meant. Because Paul mentioned angels in this Epistle, the following possibilities may get us thinking in the right direction.

► **Possibility # 1**

In l Corinthians 4:9 and 13:1, angels are mentioned alongside *anthropos*, the gender-inclusive word for human beings. It seems he was contrasting humans, who have gender distinctions and angels, who seemingly do not.

I Corinthians 4:9
For I think that God hath set forth us the apostles last, as it were appointed to death: for we are made a spectacle unto the world, and to angels, and to men.

I Corinthians 13:1a
Though I speak with the tongues of men and of angels, ...

Jesus taught that after the Resurrection we will not marry but we will be "like the angels in heaven." Either we will no longer have gender or our gender will be irrelevant. Perhaps Paul was reminding the Corinthian believers that because gender distinctions would not be important in eternity, we should not make such a big deal about them now.

► **Possibility # 2**

In l Corinthians 6:3, he said *"know ye not that we shall judge angels? How much more things that pertain to this life!"* Maybe this is what Paul had in mind in l Corinthians 11:10, for three verses later he commanded the Corinthians *"Judge for yourselves: is it comely* (proper) *that a woman pray unto God uncovered?"* Perhaps Paul was simply saying, you're going to judge angels someday. Surely you can make responsible choices about what to wear on your head now.

Authority Not Independence

Paul then went on in verse ll to remind both men and women that for them, all God-given rights and authority had to be exercised in cooperation, not in independence. Keep in mind that Paul was writing this in the context of discussing public worship. His words opposed the pagan practice of excluding women in worship, and the synagogue practice of relegating women to a side chamber or a balcony as silent observers as men worship. Exclusion based on gender was to be unheard of among the redeemed of the Christ. Ministry was to be shared.

Another important thing to notice is that in verse ll when

Paul said "in the Lord," he wasn't limiting equality to church or worship. Everything we do throughout the week, in our homes, in the workplace, as well as in our places of worship, is "in the Lord." The idea of separating the sacred from the secular is not a biblical idea.

Freedom from centuries of oppression was to begin with the house of God, then permeate society. Jesus inaugurated and Paul promoted a whole new order of equality in the world not known since Genesis 3. The aim was to restore God's original plan; the partnership for which He created men and women.

In closing Paul returned once again to our creation as human beings, restating how we depend on one another. *(Read verse 12)* Because we have interdependent origins, we shouldn't be sniping at one another, despising one another, or feeling superior or excluding one another. There is no place for this in the family of God, according to Paul. In the Lord, the sex war is over.

Luke 19:10
For the Son of man is come to seek and to save that which was lost.

Lesson 10

Praying & Prophesying

Praying and Prophesying

l Corinthians 11:4-7
4. Every man praying or prophesying, having his head covered, dishonoureth his head.
5. But every woman that prayeth or prophesieth with her head uncovered dishonoureth her head: for that is even all one as if she were shaven.
6. For if the woman be not covered, let her also be shorn: but if it be a shame for a woman to be shorn or shaven, let her be covered.
7. For a man indeed ought not to cover his head, forasmuch as he is the image and glory of God: but the woman is the glory of the man.

These verses not only speak of hairdos and attire but also contain some of the clearest statements supporting women in public ministry. Paul expected men and women to participate together in the ministry of the church.

Let's not overlook the obvious. Paul talked about appropriate attire for those who ministered in public in the Corinthian church. These are not absolute commandments for all times and all places, as some have preached.

Before we look at what these hair fashions meant in first - century Corinth, we should note the obvious thing about this passage: Paul told both men and women what to wear while ministering in public, because he expected both men and women to minister in public.

The Full Scope Of Ministry

"To pray and to prophesy" summarized the full scope of the Jewish concept of priestly ministry. To pray is to speak to God on behalf of people, and to prophesy is to speak to people on behalf of God. Prayer may be private or public, but prophesy is almost always public. Because of Paul's statements to men and women in this passage, it is clear that a woman's ministry of prayer and prophecy is as public as a man's.

Prophecy is more than predicting the future with the help of the Holy Spirit. Paul showed how broad prophecy could be.

l Corinthians 14:3
But everyone who prophesieth speaketh unto men to edification, and exhortation, and comfort.

It could also be defined as preaching or proclaiming.

Paul assumed that women, as well as, men would be prophesying. In fact women prophesying alongside men was to be a feature of the church, according to the prophet Joel. On the day the church was born, that's exactly what happened as those filled with the Spirit, all 120 men and women, began to minister publicly. Peter reminded their audience this was supposed to happen, quoting Joel's words ... Your sons and your daughters will prophesy.

Paul didn't think women were "second-best" ministers. No, he treated them as peers in preaching the Gospel. If Paul had intended to prohibit women from public ministry, he wouldn't have taken time to correct the manner in which they were ministering. Why would Paul spend time pruning a custom that he wanted to uproot?

Whom Did Paul Correct?

Paul spent almost equal time correcting men and women for improper attire.

Why did Paul show such concern about fashion? Does God really care how long someone's hair is or whether a woman wears a hat in church? As we listen to Paul's side of an imaginary phone conversation, it's impossible to say with certainty what was going on in the Corinthian church in this regard. We can't be absolutely sure what abuses Paul was dealing with. The church in Corinth was an incredible melting pot of ethnic groups, social classes, and converts from a wide variety of religions. For each of these groups, men and women's hairstyles were different and what people wore on their heads held different meanings.

Hats On, Hats Off

Jewish men usually wore their hair long and covered their heads when in the synagogue. Most of the religious, kept heads covered at all times. Jewish married women kept their long hair covered, for the rabbis taught that a woman's long hair was sexually enticing.

Greek men, on the other hand, could wear their hair long or short, though at this time the style was generally short. Heads were always uncovered. Long hair was considered a sign of beauty for Greek women, who kept their heads covered in public.

Roman men wore their hair short and uncovered, but like

the Jews, they covered their heads in worship. Roman women had a wide variety of hairstyles and head coverings. (Statues had changeable hairdos because they changed so often). Generally speaking, the Romans regarded the veil as a sign of a free, married woman and wouldn't allow any slave or former prostitute the right to wear the attire of the aristocrats.

Prostitutes in apostolic times were known to advertise themselves by means of their uncovered heads, "an invitation to lust." This would have been a common sight in Corinth, a city famous for its army of harlots.

Gender reversals were also part of several pagan religions. One of these was the cult of Dionysus. In this religion, men dressed as women with long hair and veils and women cut their hair short and wore men's clothing. All this was the mix of the church in Corinth.

What was Paul addressing in l Corinthians 11? Were ex-prostitutes worshiping Jesus the same way they had worshiped Aphrodite, with heads uncovered? Was Paul telling men not to wear their hair long or cover their heads because some were cross -dressing, as they had done in Worship of Dionysus? Or could Paul have insisted on women wearing veils as a way of giving honor to slave women and ex-prostitutes, who would have been denied that right in Corinth? Did Paul tell the men not to cover their heads in worship as an outward sign that they were no longer under Jewish law or worshiping as Roman men did? Perhaps it's not necessary to recreate all the precise historical issues when it comes to Corinthian hair do's and don'ts. Paul made it very clear that this teaching was dependent on the particular culture. If it is not a shame in your culture, it doesn't apply. Again let's look at verse 6

I Corinthians 11:6
For if the woman be not covered, let her also be shorn: but if it be a shame for a woman to be shorn or shaven, let her be covered.

She's That And More

Paul concluded this section of his letter by saying that a man should uncover his head when he ministers because "he is the image and glory of God; but the woman is the Glory of man." What is this about? Did Paul mean that only man and not woman, was made in the image and glory of God? Did Paul limit the image and glory of God to the male? What Paul was actually saying was, woman is the glory of God and of man.

The Great Affirmation Of Women

He wasn't saying that the male is the glory of God in contrast to the female, who is not. That's impossible for God didn't glory in his creation until He had made the female to join the male, God looked at the male standing there alone and said, "It is not good." Only when the two stood together as partners did God exclaim, "It is very good." Since Paul referred to this exact episode two verses later in verse 9, he clearly had this in mind.

I Corinthians 11:9
Neither was the man created for the woman; but the woman for the man.

We would be right in paraphrasing this verse as, "Whereas the male is the glory of God along with the female, the female is also the glory of the male." Paul was showing the men of Corinth that even as Adam gloried in Eve's creation, breaking into song when he first saw her, they should glory in the women who ministered in their midst. Women weren't dishonorable inferiors to be used or avoided, as the Greeks, Romans and Jews taught. They were valuable, even glorious peers and should be treated respectfully, as full partners in ministry. Paul was telling the men not to despise the women, but to value, honor, and appreciate the women who ministered in their midst. This is one of the most affirming phrases about women in Scriptures.

Two Things To Notice In Paul's Postscript

I Corinthians 11:13-15
13. Judge in yourselves: is it comely that a woman pray unto God uncovered?
14. Doth not even nature itself teach you, that, if a man have long hair, it is a shame unto him?
15. But if a woman have long hair, it is a glory to her: for her hair is given her for a covering.

Let's notice two things. First, Paul began with the imperative "Judge for yourselves." There is only one imperative in this passage and it is directed to both males and females without distinction. Paul didn't want blind obedience. He wanted people to become spiritually mature and make responsible decisions based on the principles he had already given. He posed questions, but didn't give prepackaged answers. He wanted them to make up their own minds about what to wear while ministering.

Second, what does the phrase *"Doth not even nature"* or as some translate it "Does not the very nature of things" mean in relation to men and women having long hair? Paul couldn't have meant that physical nature teaches this. Physical nature teaches a man if he doesn't visit a barber, his hair will grow long. Is that a shame or glory? Obviously, Paul must have had something else in mind other than some absolute, universal hair code. Paul was talking about culture, about what was considered natural in Corinthian society at that time.

Keep in mind that in verse 6, Paul didn't say a woman should cover her head no matter what. He said to do so "if it is a shame ..." On the one hand, Paul's teaching radically challenged and transformed culture by means of the Gospel." On the other hand, Paul didn't ignore culture; he was very respectful of people and their culture. He had pointed that out in l Corinthians 10:31.

I Corinthians 10:31
Whether therefore ye eat, or drink, or whatsoever ye do, do all to the glory of God.

(Let's include or substitute in verse 31 "cover your head or leave it bare, have long hair or have short hair.")

Pray And Prophesy

Paul wrapped it up by saying, *"If any man seems to be contentious about this, we have no such custom (or practice) neither the churches of God."* What was Paul referring to when he said, "we have no other practice"? Was he talking about women having long hair or wearing something on their heads in church? That seems highly unlikely since he had just told them to judge for themselves what to wear in ministry.

Paul was talking about men and women both praying and prophesying in public. Ministering as coworkers in Christ. He was defending this practice, giving women rights that Corinthian culture had denied them. The practice the churches of God upheld, was men and women sharing in the ministry of the church equal before God and yet completely interdependent.

This is the practice we are to embrace without contention, for the Gospel of Jesus Christ calls for men and women to minister side by side.

So, Should Women Keep Silent?

l Corinthians 14:34
Let your women keep silence in the churches: for it is not permitted unto them to speak; but they are commanded to be under obedience, as also saith the law.

If you bring up the subject of women preachers, many Christians quote this. If Paul was saying that women should not minister publicly, he was contradicting what he said earlier when he gave instructions for women's dress code while prophesying.

Paul was definitely not teaching against women ministering publicly. Rather, he was correcting, the way in which women were ministering in the Corinthian church, specifically.

In fact, verses 26-40 are all about both men and women in Corinth learning how to minister. Paul's main idea was that since God is a God of order, all should participate in Christian worship in an orderly and edifying way. He then proceeded to illustrate this principle by giving examples of what orderly worship should look like. The examples he chose were those who speak in tongues, those who prophesy and the women of the church.

I Corinthians 14:26-40
26. How is it then, brethren? when ye come together, every one of you hath a psalm, hath a doctrine, hath a tongue, hath a revelation, hath an interpretation. Let all things be done unto edifying.
27. If any man speak in an unknown tongue, let it be by

two, or at the most by three, and that by course; and let one interpret.
28. But if there be no interpreter, let him keep silence in the church; and let him speak to himself, and to God.
29. Let the prophets speak two or three, and let the other judge.
30. If any thing be revealed to another that sitteth by, let the first hold his peace.
31. For ye may all prophesy one by one, that all may learn, and all may be comforted.
32. And the spirits of the prophets are subject to the prophets.
33. For God is not the author of confusion, but of peace, as in all churches of the saints.
34. Let your women keep silence in the churches: for it is not permitted unto them to speak; but they are commanded to be under obedience, as also saith the law.
35. And if they will learn any thing, let them ask their husbands at home: for it is a shame for women to speak in the church.
36. What? came the word of God out from you? or came it unto you only?
37. If any man think himself to be a prophet, or spiritual, let him acknowledge that the things that I write unto you are the commandments of the Lord.
38. But if any man be ignorant, let him be ignorant.
39. Wherefore, brethren, covet to prophesy, and forbid not to speak with tongues.
40. Let all things be done decently and in order.

Paul's first word to women was corrective. *(Read again: verses 34-35 above).* Over the years Paul's command to the women to be silent has been the focal point of much discussion. However many overlook the important fact that this command does not stand alone. Paul had already given the exact same command to be silent twice in this very passage. He had told to be silent various individuals and groups who were disrupting the service. Each of these three commands was given so that the Corinthian worship would reflect the character of a "God of peace" and result in the edification of all present.

Paul hammered home again and again the message to remain silent. However, we have lost the impact of his deliberate repetition of the one command by the way it has been translated:

- Those who speak in tongues *"let him keep silence" (v. 28)*
- The prophets *"hold his peace" (v.30)*
- The women *"keep silence" (v.34)*

These appear to be three different commands, but they are not. Paul repeated the exact same word in Greek to each group. He intended us to see a deliberate continuity of thought between verses 28, 30, and 34. To see the symmetry of Paul's repetition restored, we should translate the text as follows:

- To those who speak in tongues "be silent" (v.28)
- To the prophets "be silent" (v.30)
- To the women "be silent" (v.34)

It is dishonest to single out the command directed to the women and make it more of an absolute than the command given to those who speak in tongues or to the prophets. Why have some been obsessed with the third example of orderly conduct and ignored the first two?

It's obvious Paul's "be silent" wasn't an "absolutely-forever-under-every-circumstance-and-at-all-times" injunction against those who spoke in tongues or those who prophesied. No, in the same passage he wrote in *verse 39: covet* (or be eager) *to prophesy and forbid not to speak with tongues.* The ministry gifts were not to be permanently silenced but were to be exercised *"decently and in order" (verse 40).* Paul was not telling women to refrain from all public ministry. To force such an interpretation does violence to the integrity of the text.

Paul Linked Being Silent To Taking Turns

In these verses "be silent" had to do with taking turns, listening to one another and being self-controlled "so that everyone may be instructed and encouraged" *(verse 31).* Those who spoke in tongues and the prophets were to participate at times and be silent at times so that all might be done for the strengthening of the church *(verse 26).* The same would be true for the women of the church.

Considering this passage carefully, we see that prior to verse 34, women had already been told to be silent. Women were most probably among those who spoke in tongues and they were most definitely among those who prophesied. So when Paul earlier instructed the first two groups to be silent, he was not speaking to a group comprising only male ministers. In fact, the gender-inclusive nature of the church's ministry is clear throughout the passage. "Everyone" knew no gender limitations.

When you think about it, the fact that Paul was having to correct the women in the "way" they were ministering confirms the fact that they "were" ministering. If Paul hadn't given them freedom to minister in the first place, they couldn't have ministered wrongly. It was because they did not know how to exercise this freedom correctly that they now stood in need of his correction.

Why Was Paul Correcting The Women?

Several possible reasons exist for Paul's words *"Let your*

women keep silence"

► Women like the men, may have been ministering without consideration for others lacking self-control.

► Because women were uneducated they may have been interrupting the services by asking questions.

► Some of the women may have been reverting to the model of their pagan worship, disrupting the service with their loud noises.

In pagan religions, the only way women were allowed to participate was by wailing and making high-pitched cries called "ululations." Among pagans, the men ministered and offered sacrifices while the women provided the sound effects. Paul now expected all to minister, but in an orderly way, without the chaos of their pagan past.

Paul Told The Women To Speak Too

The purpose of this passage was not to limit ministry but to encourage it. Paul wanted to teach new believers how to minister in this young church. He had already said he wanted all men and women to be ready to contribute with "a psalm, a doctrine, a tongue, an interpretation." Paul found it necessary to correct wrong forms of ministry with his three "be silents." The primary objective was to get the people to minister. This is why he also commanded these people to "speak." There is no indication in the text that these three commands to speak were limited to men.

Submit Or Be Under Obedience To Whom?

"As also sayeth the law," clearly rules out the possibility of marriage here, because nowhere in the Old Testament do we find any instruction for wives to submit to their husbands.

Some might point to Genesis 3:16.

Genesis 3:16
Unto the woman he said, I will greatly multiply thy sorrow and thy conception; in sorrow thou shalt bring forth children; and thy desire shall be to thy husband, and he shall rule over thee.

But we've already seen God was just describing the consequences of sin. God never intended Genesis 3:16 to become our guide for life and relationships

Paul did not specify to whom or to what women were to be under obedience or submission. This omission is quite surprising when we see that out of the 38 places in the New Testament where this verb *(upotasso)* appears, this is the only time the object 'to whom to submit' is not clearly stated. The only instance!

Of course, some have assumed that Paul meant husbands, so want to rush ahead to the next verse. But up to this point husband-and-wife relationships haven't been mentioned at all in this passage. This is the conclusion of a seven-part series on public worship in the church. Up to now marriage has not been the subject of the discussion, but ministry has been.

So to whom or to what were these women to submit? Three good possibilities stand out: (1) the church, (2) God, and (3) themselves.

► Possibility 1: The Churches

The last noun mentioned was the churches. If this is what Paul meant, he was telling the women to be submissive to the order of the church or to the leaders of the church as they exercised their ministry gifts. The same as those speaking in tongues or prophesying were to do, so that worship could be done in an orderly, edifying way.

▶ Possibility 2: God

Looking further back, the next noun is God, when Paul said *"God is not the author of confusion, but of peace."* We are all supposed to give Him unqualified submission whatever our gender. The implication would be that submitting to God would result in imitating Him, bringing order and peace to correct whatever was going on in the Corinthian church during worship.

It's interesting to see the phrase "orderly way" in verse 40 and "submit" come from the same root word in Greek. Paul was saying that order cannot reign in the church unless everyone has a submissive attitude.

▶ Possibility 3: Themselves

I Corinthians 14:32
And the spirits of the prophets are subject to the prophets.

Self-control was supposed to characterize the exercise of spiritual gifts. Prophetic utterances of the Spirit of God were completely different from the uncontrollable outbursts of pagan worship. The prophet was to keep his or her spirit in submission. Again, women weren't the first group Paul required to submit in this way. Paul expected to find such submission in the life of anyone who ministered in the church.

What Law Was Paul Referring To?

I began this by saying "as also sayeth the law," rules out husbands. So considering these 3 possibilities: to the church, to God, or to themselves, only one emerges with a clear Old Testament foundation. Psalms 37:7 commands *"Rest in the Lord," (be silent to the Lord) and wait patiently for Him. (KJV)* It is interesting to note how this verse was translated in the Septuagint.

The Greek - speaking Jews who prepared a Greek version of the Hebrew Bible (The Septuagint) saw a remarkable correlation between "silence" and "submission."

There are three places in Psalms where the Hebrew text speaks of being silent unto God. In each case ... translators rendered this by the Greek verb meaning "to submit oneself." This implication is attentiveness and receptivity to God."

Look at Psalm 62, verse 1 ...
Psalms 62:1, 5
1. Truly my soul waiteth upon God: from him cometh my salvation.

... and also verse 5.

5. My soul, wait thou only upon God; for my expectation is from him.

Perhaps when he spoke of submission, Paul simply had in mind the Old Testament idea of "waiting on God," or the thought of humility toward God. If so, Paul was saying to the women, "you've been given the privilege of ministering in the church: The double standard is over, you have new freedom in Christ. However, we expect the same thing from you that we expect from the men. You must minister responsibly. Stop ministering in a disorderly, disruptive, discourteous, insubordinate way. Your participation in the church must be done in an orderly way, submitting to God so that your ministry edifies the whole Body of Christ."

Paul Does A Really Cool Thing

Next Paul encourages the women in their desire to learn.

I Corinthians 14:35a
And if they will learn any thing, let them ask their husbands at home:...

He was urging them not to stay on the sidelines, but to equip themselves for full participation in the Body of Christ! This was radical, as women had little or no educational opportunities among the Greeks, Romans, or Jews.

Paul would have no part of this exclusion. He affirmed a woman's right to learn. However women were to ask these questions in an appropriate setting, not during the worship service, interrupting while someone else was praying, prophesying, or otherwise publicly ministering.

Men had never been given the obligation to provide their wives with any kind of education; not since the beginning of time! It was up to the husbands of the church in Corinth to re-orient their values and spend the time necessary to bring their wives up to speed. If their wives wanted to learn, they should do everything they could to help them.

Paul was making sure the women were not left out. They were at a disadvantage. Because of their cultures, women were entering the Kingdom of God with an educational handicap. Paul's instructions sought to eradicate that.

This was no small thing. He was giving women the tools to enter into their God-ordained destinies. His words showed Paul's compassionate leadership, opening new doors of opportunity for those whom society had excluded and ignored.

Paul Defended Women In Ministry

Paul took up the challenge of the statement *"It is a shame for women to speak in the church."* The Greek word translated "shame or disgraceful" occurs only three times in the New Testament. The fact that Paul used it both here and in the first difficult passage we considered, helps us interpret it.

I Corinthians 11:7b, we saw how Paul in the context of women praying and prophesying went to great lengths to affirm that women were; the glory of men; a source of joy; not of embarrassment (becuase of pride); not of dishonor.

I Corinthians 11:7b
... but the woman is the glory of the man.

Clearly, this statement; that women speaking in the church was disgraceful, was not something that Paul endorsed.

Paul told women to be silent, but not because the fact that what they were speaking was disgraceful. Their speaking was contributing to disorder in the church and standing in the way of people being edified: Paul didn't make women taboo. He made chaos taboo.

The critics of women participating in the Corinthian church had totally missed Paul's point. They were holding to old concepts from Greek, Roman and Jewish culture, not to things taught by Christ. See how closely this statement quoted by Paul mirrored the pervasive thoughts of the ancients:

- The Greeks said, -"The women in silence obey."

- Aristotle: -"Silence gives grace to woman."
- The Romans: -"Keeping at home and keeping silence" was the appropriate role for women, or "A woman's always worth more seen than heard."
- Jewish Rabbis: -"Thy silence is fairer than thy speech." or "A silent wife gift of the Lord." or -"A woman's voice is a sexual incitement, therefore to listen to a woman's voice is indecent.

Paul Says "No Way!"

What, then was Paul's response to this dredging up of the old idea that it was disgraceful for women to speak? Paul countered ("Nonsense!") What! Did the Word of God originate with you? What! Are you the only people it has reached?

In other words, Paul refuted the claim of some men to hold exclusive rights to minister. Paul had already established the validity of women in public ministry and wasn't going to allow anyone to contradict him on this point. *(Read verses 37-38)*

I Corinthians 14:37-38
37. If any man think himself to be a prophet, or spiritual, let him acknowledge that the things that I write unto you are the commandments of the Lord.
38. But if any man be ignorant, let him be ignorant.

He then returned to the other two groups, defending their right to minister as well. Finished with the central theme in verse 40. So, should women "be silent"? Yes, like the men. Should women be prepared to minister? Yes, just like the men. Should women exercise self-control as they minister? Yes, just like the men. Should women seek to educate themselves so that they can better edify others when they minister? Yes, just like the men. *"For God is not the author of confusion but of peace."*

How ironic that some have actually been using a statement written by a group of 1st-century legalists - men who wanted to burden the New Testament church with stifling Jewish rules and traditions, to shackle Christian women who are called to liberty in the Holy Spirit. Whom do we want to follow; the apostle Paul, who invited women to preach, pray, and prophesy in the church; or the legalists, who believed that it was "obscene" for women to speak in public?

This verse is too often used to put a bit and bridle in the mouths of godly Christian women: it was never intended to keep females from teaching the Bible, proclaiming the gospel or aggressively sharing their faith. How ridiculous! Didn't the Holy Spirit fall on all the believers on the Day of Pentecost? On that day, weren't the women, as well as, the men empowered to be a witness of His Resurrection. Didn't Peter remind them in Acts 2:17 of the Prophet Joel's prediction that *"your sons and your daughters will prophesy"*?

Weren't all Jesus' followers, male and female, commanded to go into all the world to make disciples and teach all nations?

Matthew 28:19-20
19. Go ye therefore, and teach all nations, baptizing them in the name of the Father, and of the Son, and of the Holy Ghost:
20. Teaching them to observe all things whatsoever I have commanded you: and, lo, I am with you alway, even unto the end of the world. Amen.

Some have overlooked the obvious message of the Bible and then taken one obscure passage from Paul's writings and twisted it to keep women in a place of subjugation and insignificance. I'm sure the devil has laughed in delight, at the way some have actually helped him silence the spreading of the gospel! By telling, women that it is virtuous for them to sit in the back of the church with their mouths closed, they've been kept out of the pulpits and off the mission fields. Wonder how many people have gone to Hell, because no one preached the Gospel to them because a woman wasn't allowed.

What if Evangelist Aimee Semple McPherson had swallowed the lie that women should not speak in church? She never would have blazed a trail across the U.S. in the 1920's with her Pentecostal message, and she never would have started the International Church of the Foursquare Gospel, a denomination with nearly a half-million members in Latin America alone in 1999.

May God forgive all the men who hinder the spread of the Gospel through called and anointed women of God by telling them they can't obey His call. May the truth be preached and taught with boldness to both men and women, by both men and women.

Galatians 3:28
There is neither Jew nor Greek, there is neither bond nor free, there is neither male nor female: for ye are all one in Christ Jesus.

Lesson 11

Women Teachers?

"But I Suffer Not A Woman To Teach"

I Timothy 2:1-15
1. I exhort therefore, that, first of all, supplications, prayers, intercessions, and giving of thanks, be made for all men;
2. For kings, and for all that are in authority; that we may lead a quiet and peaceable life in all godliness and honesty.
3. For this is good and acceptable in the sight of God our Saviour;
4. Who will have all men to be saved, and to come unto the knowledge of the truth.
5. For there is one God, and one mediator between God and men, the man Christ Jesus;
6. Who gave himself a ransom for all, to be testified in due time.
7. Whereunto I am ordained a preacher, and an apostle, (I speak the truth in Christ, and lie not;) a teacher of the Gentiles in faith and verity.
8. I will therefore that men pray every where, lifting up holy hands, without wrath and doubting.
9. In like manner also, that women adorn themselves in modest apparel, with shamefacedness and sobriety; not with broided hair, or gold, or pearls, or costly array;
10. But (which becometh women professing godliness) with good works.
11. Let the woman learn in silence with all subjection.
12. But I suffer not a woman to teach, nor to usurp authority over the man, but to be in silence.

13. For Adam was first formed, then Eve.
14. And Adam was not deceived, but the woman being deceived was in the transgression.
15. Notwithstanding she shall be saved in childbearing, if they continue in faith and charity and holiness with sobriety.

Now let's look at the third difficult passage regarding women in ministry. We must first understand the situation Paul was addressing if we are to understand what he was saying to his protégé Timothy. Paul was writing sometime between his first and second imprisonment in Rome. It had been almost ten years since he had founded the church in Ephesus, which Timothy was now pastoring.

Persecution From Without Heresy Within

As Paul wrote his first letter to Timothy the church at Ephesus was undergoing tremendous difficulties. The Jews and pagan religious leaders continued persecuting it. As if that weren't enough false teachers within the church were promoting heresy. Timothy definitely had his hands full!

Overview of Timothy

As we read through this Epistle of Paul to his "true son in the faith," two things stand out

- ► Paul's concern for Timothy
- ► Paul's concern for the church at Ephesus

What Paul Thought Most Important

The first Epistle to Timothy took shape as Paul alternated between his concern for Timothy and his concern for the church. It's clear, however, that Paul emphasized one thing more than any other. In 1 Timothy 2:1 through 1 Timothy 4:5 Paul poured out his concern for the church at Ephesus. It is within this section that we find 1 Timothy 2:1-15.

The overall principle is that God wants to save everyone. Then we see examples of what God wants to do with men and women. Within the last example, women, Paul began talking about women in general, them switched to a particular woman, then switched back to women in general.

What was Paul saying here? Was he really saying that women should not teach, here in a church where Priscilla had been a founding leader? A church where she had spent much time along with her husband Aquila, correcting the early errors of Apollos, discipling him for leadership? Was Paul, who had asked the church in Rome to receive the woman minister Phoebe with all due honor, now contradicting himself, telling Timothy never to allow women to be leaders in the church?

Let's first look at the very important foundation that Paul laid in the first seven verses of I Timothy 2.

1 Timothy 2:1-7
1. I exhort therefore, that, first of all, supplications, prayers, intercessions, and giving of thanks, be made for all men;
2. For kings, and for all that are in authority; that we may lead a quiet and peaceable life in all godliness and honesty.
3. For this is good and acceptable in the sight of God our Saviour;
4. Who will have all men to be saved, and to come unto the knowledge of the truth.
5. For there is one God, and one mediator between God and men, the man Christ Jesus;
6. Who gave himself a ransom for all, to be testified in due time.

7.Whereunto I am ordained a preacher, and an apostle, (I speak the truth in Christ, and lie not;) a teacher of the Gentiles in faith and verity.

Gods's Forever Dream

Paul began this passage saying *"I exhort therefore that first of all ..."* Therefore linked what Paul had just said with what was to come.

In l Timothy 1, we see a Church in deep trouble. Persecutors without and false teachers were wrecking havoc within. The natural tendency would be to withdraw, but Paul said it was time to be proactive. It was time to pray.

Paul urged the believers at Ephesus to pray in every possible way! No one was to be excluded from their prayers either.

Why pray so intensely? Paul said, "*... that we may lead a quiet and peaceful life in all godliness and holiness.*"

The Greek word for quiet that Paul used will be a key to understand verses later on in this chapter. It summed up the desired goal for all believers male and female.

Throughout this first seven verses of l Timothy 2, Paul did not use *'aner'*, the Greek word for "men." Instead he used *'anthropos'*, the gender - inclusive word best translated as "person" or "humans."

Why is this important? Paul was going out of his way to make it clear that God's love was for every human being. Jesus became a human so that He could be a mediator for every man and woman. Woman was an equal recipient of God's love and Jesus' extravagant sacrifice.

What a shame some have rushed past these words to tackle difficult issues raised later. They miss the intimate glimpse into the heart of God's love. But they also, misunderstand the words that follow. For unless we keep this perspective of God's forever dream before us, we miss it all.

Paul Talked To The Men

He turned to the men and told them their part in verse 8. For the first time in this passage, he used the Greek word for "males," aner. He told the men what he wanted to see in their lives. They were to pray in the opposite spirit of those attacking the church from without and from within. The men of the church were to live differently than both the unredeemed pagans persecuting them and the unrepentant teachers of heresy.

Next, Paul Spoke to all the Women; 'A Woman,' then all the Women

First he spoke to the women in general, then he gave specific instructions to one woman, then he spoke again to all the women. He began in verse 9-10.

He begins with "likewise" or "in the same way." This word in the Greek is like a literary equal sign. Paul deliberately chose this word to highlight the similarities, not differences, of men and women's roles. It is implied or suggested that Paul wanted both men and women to pray and to live in such a way that they promoted God's forever dream.

He wanted the men to pray and in the same way he wanted the women to pray. He told both groups to pray in a godly manner - men in holiness and without anger, and women, with decency and propriety. (Or in a becoming manner.)

Why the Fuss over Gold, Pearls, and Braided Hair?

Just as Paul urged the men to live their lives by a different standard, here he was warning the women to avoid things that would detract from their witness. We've seen that Ephesus was a sensuous, immoral city. Furthermore in N.T. times, ostentatious dress in itself was considered a mark of promiscuity. Wearing pearls was considered the most ostentatious display of vanity in that time. Paul wanted Christian women to live in a way that was "appropriate for women who profess to worship God."

The word profess is key within this passage. In the original, it conveys a sense of proclamation, profession and expertise. In fact, it is one of eight Greek verbs in the New Testament formed by adding a prefix to the word for messenger. All of these verbs have to do with communication. Paul used seven of the eight in his letters.

- to tell
- to announce
- to herald
- to profess
- to evangelize
- to proclaim
- to declare

The word profess and its linguistic cousins are linked to the very heart and soul of Christian ministry. You can't profess something in silence, nor can you profess something in private. He was showing that the women were involved in public ministry, communicating the Gospel to others.

A False Teacher Silenced

Now in l Timothy 2:11-15a, Paul changed his tone and the focus of his attention, He spoke to a particular woman.

I Timothy 2:11-15a
11. Let the woman learn in silence with all subjection.

12. But I suffer not a woman to teach, nor to usurp authority over the man, but to be in silence.
13. For Adam was first formed, then Eve.
14. And Adam was not deceived, but the woman being deceived was in the transgression.
15a. Notwithstanding she shall be saved in childbearing, ...

In verse 10, Paul spoke to the women involved in spreading the Gospel. As he did so, he remembered one woman who had perhaps played a prominent role in the church at Ephesus. So, in verse 11, he stopped speaking in broad, general terms ("everyone," "men," and "women") and addressed the case of this one woman. How can we say that? This is based on a very clear grammatical shift in the Greek. From verse 11 to the middle of verse 15, the plural nouns are gone. They're all singular: *"a woman," "she must be silent."* and *"she shall be saved through the childbearing."* Then in the second half of verse 15, Paul returned to the plural, *"if they."*

- verses 9-10: women (plural)
- verses 10-15a: a woman (singular)
- verses 15b: woman (plural)

Why did Paul make this dramatic shift from plural to singular and back to plural? The context suggests that he had a specific Ephesian woman in mind who was a vocal promoter of the false teachings troubling the Ephesian church. Perhaps she was one of the leaders of this heretical group. Several other clues point strongly to such a scenario.

- **Clue # 1 The Pronoun Paul Used**

In several places where Paul told Timothy to deal with false teachers, he used gender-inclusive pronouns indicating women were also involved: *(Ref: l Tim. 1:6, 4:1, 6:3, 21)* l Timothy 1:3b Paul told Timothy to silence false teachers; male and female.

I Timothy 1:3b
... that thou mightest charge some that they teach no other doctrine,

- **Clue # 2 Women Involved in Heresies**

In I Timothy 4 Paul urged Timothy to refuse *"old wives' tales,"* which suggest older women were among the false teachers.

I Timothy 4:7
But refuse profane and old wives' fables, and exercise thyself rather unto godliness.

Then later in Chapter 5 verse 13, we see the younger women were swept in too: young widows were *"saying things they ought not to."*

I Timothy 5:13
And withal they learn to be idle, wandering about from house to house; and not only idle, but tattlers also and busybodies, speaking things which they ought not.

Paul said that women who had succumbed to the false teaching were "silly (weak-willed) women.

ll Timothy 3:6-7
6. For of this sort are they which creep into houses, and lead captive silly women laden with sins, led away with divers lusts,
7. Ever learning, and never able to come to the knowledge of the truth.

Obviously, Paul did not see heresy as the domain of one gender. Both men and women *(Anthropos)* had participated in the heresy that was tearing the Ephesian church apart.

II Timothy 3:13
But evil men (original text *'Anthropos') and seducers shall wax worse and worse, deceiving, and being deceived.*

- **Clue # 3 False Teachers, Named and Unnamed**

Though Paul spoke of a group that had been led astray, he also referred to several individuals most responsible for this deception:

- Hymenaeus *(Ref: l Tim. 1:20, ll Tim. 2:17)*
- Alexander *(Ref: l Tim. 1:20; ll Tim. 4:14-15)*
- Philetus *(Ref: ll Tim. 2:17)*

Why didn't Paul mention the woman by name? There were other times when he didn't mention an individual by name, but made it clear about whom he was talking. He did this when writing to the church in Corinth about a man committing incest *(See: l Cor. 5:1 and 5)* and when writing to Titus concerning an unnamed, yet specific person.

Titus 3:10-11
10. A man that is an heretick after the first and second admonition reject;
11. Knowing that he that is such is subverted, and sinneth, being condemned of himself.

The context suggests that Paul had a particular person in mind. Like Timothy in Ephesus, Titus had been left in Crete to "straighten out what was left unfinished" *(Ref: Titus 1:5)* and confront a group of false teachers who, according to Paul "must be stopped" or "silenced."

Titus 1:11
Whose mouths must be stopped, who subvert whole houses,

teaching things which they ought not, for filthy lucre's sake.

Paul didn't mention by name the ringleader because they both knew who was at the heart of the problem in Crete. *(Ref: Titus 3: 10-11)*

Perhaps Paul did not name the contentious person in Crete, the man committing incest in Corinth, or the woman teaching heresy in Ephesus because he hoped they would be restored.

It isn't surprising that Paul told Timothy to silence this woman without naming her. Perhaps he had given up on Hymenaeus, Alexander, and Philetus.

- **Clue # 4 Back to Eve**

Paul gave the reason this woman should be silenced by immediately pointing to another deceived woman, Eve.

Paul explained what Timothy was to do with this deceived woman. Then, just to make it clear to him, Paul used the word 'for' or 'because' to compare her situation to that of Eve in the Garden. Paul reminded Timothy that Adam sinned with his eyes wide open, but Eve did so because she was deceived. Paul held Adam more accountable for his sin because he wasn't deceived when he decided to disobey God. *(See also: Ro. 5:12-21; l Cor. 15:22)* One of the major themes of this entire passage was stopping the deception in the Ephesian church. Eve and this woman who were to be silenced had both been deceived. Both were acting on false beliefs.

What these two women had in common was that they both believed a lie. As a result they both had sinned. The sin of both had affected the lives of a large number of people in a very negative way.

Paul wanted to put an end to the conditions that made

deception possible. He understood that the women of his day were more prone to being deceived because they had been excluded from education opportunities. Paul intended to put an end to this deception.

The three men had been turned over to Satan. But he handed the woman over to a teacher. Which would you prefer?

Paul went on to say how she should learn: *"in silence and subjection"* or closer to the original Greek "in quietness and full submission."

The phrase "silence and submission" was a frequent formula for a model student. In Paul's time the rabbis agreed that silence was an admirable attribute for the pious scholar.

Another thing to note is the way the Jewish rabbis linked learning and teaching: you could not have one without the other. A student was taught in order that he could teach others. Teaching was the normal end product of learning.

Paul however, commanded this woman to learn and not teach. Why? Because she had been teaching false doctrine. For this reason she was being disciplined, corrected. It was time for her to abstain from teaching altogether and dedicate herself to study.

Paul was Not Silencing Godly Women

There is nothing in this passage to support the silencing of godly women, or forbidding their teaching in church or their call to any form of Christian service. Just two verses earlier, Paul spoke of those things *"which becometh women professing godliness."* Paul expected believing women to be communicating their faith in both word and deed.

We also see Paul's attitude toward women when he reminded Timothy of his spiritual heritage.

II Timothy 1:5
When I call to remembrance the unfeigned faith that is in thee, which dwelt first in thy grandmother Lois, and thy mother Eunice; and I am persuaded that in thee also.

(See also: I Tim. 4:6; II Tim. 3:14-15)

If Paul didn't approve of women teaching the Bible, he certainly missed a golden opportunity to correct Timothy here! Instead, he put a spotlight on these two women for the important role they played teaching this future leader.

Paul Wanted Reliable Women To Teach

If Paul had intended to prohibit women in teaching ministry, he missed another great opportunity in II Timothy 2:2. If he had used the Greek word *'aner'*, "males" rather than '*anthropos*', "persons," it would have settled the issue once and for all. Those of either sex who are able to teach hereby receive a summons to make known the unsearchable riches of Jesus Christ.

What About Authority?

► Usurp: to take possession of unlawfully or by force. Violent seizing of power.

The meaning of the Greek word '*Authentein*' translated *"to have authority"* is cloudy. Why? Because it is a word that appears only once in the New Testament, making it difficult for scholars to agree on its meaning. They debate over whether it has a positive or negative meaning (such as domineering, manipulating, even murdering others). The main thing for us to note is that it is not the normal New Testament word for authority, *'exousia'*. It was an unusual word for an unusual situation.

In context, a godless woman was teaching false doctrine and leading in a harmful way. She should not be allowed to hold a position of authority in the church. She didn't meet the qualification for spiritual leadership that Paul gave Timothy. *(Study: l Tim. 3:1-13)* Because she was not above reproach, in word or deed, disciplinary action was called for.

Paul didn't say anything anywhere in his letters to Timothy about a man having authority over a woman. In fact, among the redeemed, no one is to exercise authority in an authoritarian way over another person of either gender.

Mark 10:42-45
42. But Jesus called them to him, and saith unto them, Ye know that they which are accounted to rule over the Gentiles exercise lordship over them; and their great ones exercise authority upon them.
43. But so shall it not be among you: but whosoever will be great among you, shall be your minister:
44. And whosoever of you will be the chiefest, shall be servant of all.
45. For even the Son of man came not to be ministered unto, but to minister, and to give his life a ransom for many.

Paul made it clear that false teachers were the ones trying to control people.

l Timothy 4:2-3a
2. Speaking lies in hypocrisy; having their conscience seared with a hot iron;
3a. Forbidding to marry, and commanding to abstain from meats, ...

About Eve

We've already seen how Paul compared this woman to Eve for they were both deceived. The words in l Timothy 2:13-14 could indicate one of two things:

I Timothy 2:13-14
13. For Adam was first formed, then Eve.
14. And Adam was not deceived, but the woman being deceived was in the transgression.

►**1.** Paul may have been refuting the context of the false teaching. There are indications that they were distorting the truth about how God created the world. Some taught Eve came first.

► **2.** On the other hand, Paul might have simply been referring to the way Eve was deceived.

Eve didn't become deceived because of some inherent weakness in women. No. It was because Adam didn't teach her right.

The story of Adam and Eve shows how important it is to faithfully teach others, so no one falls into deception. Paul's one command here is in: The woman must learn.

She Shall Be Saved Through The Childbearing

What does this mean? Was Paul saying that this deceived woman would be reconciled to the Lord and the church if she had a baby? If so, what would this mean for single women or childless wives? This phrase "the childbearing" isn't found any place else in the New Testament. Although a variety of interpretations have been proposed, one thing to notice is that this word isn't a verb, it's a noun.

I believe Paul was still drawing parallels with Eve, the other deceived woman who was in need of salvation. The Messiah was first promised in Genesis 3:15. And Paul repeated the promise here, saying this unnamed Ephesian woman could still be saved through Him, the promised child born to redeem all persons. Women aren't saved by getting pregnant and having babies. They're saved by the child who was born, Jesus.

Paul was talking in this passage about how men and women are redeemed, not about how they procreate. Jesus was the focus.

Paul's pastoral heart was reaching out to this particular woman in Ephesus who had caused so much trouble. Paul was saying that she could be saved through the childbearing - that is through Jesus. She must learn. What must she learn? She must learn about Jesus so that she might be fully restored to God through Him!

Women Leaders Too

I Timothy 3:1-13
1. This is a true saying, If a man desire the office of a bishop, he desireth a good work.
2. A bishop then must be blameless, the husband of one wife, vigilant, sober, of good behaviour, given to hospitality, apt to teach;
3. Not given to wine, no striker, not greedy of filthy lucre; but patient, not a brawler, not covetous;
4. One that ruleth well his own house, having his children in subjection with all gravity;
5. (For if a man know not how to rule his own house, how shall he take care of the church of God?)
6. Not a novice, lest being lifted up with pride he fall into the condemnation of the devil.
7. Moreover he must have a good report of them which are without; lest he fall into reproach and the snare of the devil.
8. Likewise must the deacons be grave, not doubletongued, not given to much wine, not greedy of filthy lucre;
9. Holding the mystery of the faith in a pure conscience.
10. And let these also first be proved; then let them use the office of a deacon, being found blameless.
11. Even so must their wives be grave, not slanderers, sober, faithful in all things.

12. Let the deacons be the husbands of one wife, ruling their children and their own houses well.
13. For they that have used the office of a deacon well purchase to themselves a good degree, and great boldness in the faith which is in Christ Jesus.

We'll see again as we look at his teaching on leadership qualifications that Paul threw the door wide open for women in public ministry.

Paul turned from dealing with an ungodly woman leader, to address what it meant to be a godly leader for both men and women.

First notice Paul once again used the word anyone when talking about those who wanted to be leaders. We could add "his or her" and "he and she" in brackets because this is the true grammar Paul used.

In Like Manner the Women

Likewise women must be grave (serious), not slanderers, sober (temperate or not extreme), faithful in all things. When Paul turned to speak to the women with leadership responsibilities, he again used the word likewise. Both here and in 1 Timothy 2:9, this word bridged his discussion as he moved from men to women. Without exception, Paul treated men and women the same, as coworkers in the Gospel. He was absolutely committed to equality. This is like a literary equal sign. What was Paul talking about? Men serving as deacons, then he turned and said. *"In like manner the women."* (*'even so'* in KJV)

Deacons and Wives

The Greek word *'gune'* that Paul used here may be translated as either "women" or "wives," just as *'aner'* can be translated as either "men" or "husbands." You have to study the context to understand which fits better. By choosing to translate *gune* for "wives," some have had to add the pronoun their and a whole phrase that is nonexistent in the Greek. ... "are to be women." This choice of words exposes a prejudice against women leaders in the church that is not found in Paul's words. One clear example of this is the NIV.

Are the women in verse 11 deacons or wives of deacons? The structure of the letter and the context of Paul's message suggest that Paul fully intended for women to serve in the leadership of the church. After all, hadn't Paul begun the ministry in this city with Priscilla and her husband Aquila? Nowhere in his writings do we see him withholding leadership responsibilities from Godly women. On the contrary, we know that he saw Phoebe as a fellow servant of the Lord, affirmed her as a deacon, and commended her as a leader of the church.

Paul did not make harsh divisions between men and women, neither in the way they are saved nor how they are released into ministry. On the contrary, after the Cross, the playing field is leveled. If we are to fulfil God's forever dream; reaching everyone with the opportunity to be reconciled to Him: every one of us must pray, profess our faith, and live peaceful and quiet lives. Every one of us should follow God's leading into whatever ministry He chooses. This is true for men and likewise for the women.

A Final Word

In this book, we have seen how the Greeks, Romans, and even Jews forged chains that would last for thousands of years saying women are a curse, that they were less valuable than men, that they were to be avoided, or at least carefully quarantined.

I trust you were able to see how dark the despair of women was, and the brightness when Jesus pierced the darkness.

As Jesus dealt with women, He was restoring God's original perspective of women. He was showing that they were not an embarrassment, not objects of lust, nor creatures to be looked down on. He simply related to them as persons created in the image of God, capable of doing things considered extraordinary in their day. He sent the woman at the well to evangelize her whole village. He had women traveling and ministering alongside Him and the 12 male disciples.

Paul followed in Jesus footsteps and affirmed the ministry of women. The apostle's treatment of women as peers and coworkers couldn't be further removed from the image of a woman-hater.

In the three difficult passages, often used to limit women in ministry we saw that Paul expected women to be fully involved in the public proclamation of the Gospel. Nowhere did Paul prohibit women from sharing in leadership, in fact he actively encouraged it. He urged men to reconsider how they valued women. He affirmed the authority of women. He opened doors of educational opportunities for women. He invited, indeed he urged all - both men and women - to be involved in the ministry of the leadership of the church in Absolute Equality.

Final Review

Do You Remember?

►1. Matthew 19:3-12 and Mark 10:2-12 Jesus was doing more than just condemning divorce. He was also commanding them not to have a double standard for men and women.

A. True

B. False

►2. Jesus broke down the dividing walls that had completely marginalized women in places of worship.

A. True

B. False

►3. In Matthew 28:19, before ascending into heaven, Jesus established a sacrament designed to include both genders of the church. This new initiation rite of the people of faith, that did away with circumcision is ______________________ .

►4. The confession that Jesus is the Christ, the Son of God, was not only made by Peter, but also by Martha, the sister of Lazarus.

A. True

B. False

►5. While speaking to an outcast Samaritan woman, Jesus for the first time - stated that He was The Messiah.

A.True

B. False

►6. Jesus treated a despised and alienated woman as He

would have treated any other person hungry for truth. She became an Evangelist to her hometown and many were saved.

A. True
B. False

►7. The Gospel evidence is clear that women ministered to and with Jesus. The verb diakoneo that describes the ministry of seven men appointed to leadership in the early church is also associated with seven women in the Gospel.

A. True
B. False

►8. The Head of the Church Himself, forbade a woman, Mary Magdalene, to preach the Resurrection.

A. True
B. False

►9. In Ephesians 5:15-23, Paul gave a measuring stick of being filled with the Spirit. Are we living a life of ________________ submission?

►10. Paul said wives were to obey their husbands at all times and in whatever situation.

A. True
B. False

►11. In Galatians 3:28, Paul declared that all distinctions and categories of people have been done away with. In Christ, all are one.

A. True
B. False

►12. Priscilla and Aquila "invited Apollos, a man already eloquent in the scriptures, into their home and expounded unto him the ways of God more perfectly." Priscilla's pupil went on to have a prominent public ministry.

A. True
B. False

►13 Because Paul believed the assessment of the condition of God's people sent by one of the leaders in the Corinthian church, we have the book of 1 Corinthians.

►14. Paul told the Roman believers to help Phoebe. Just as he stood with Phoebe, he wanted them to stand with her and assist her in whatever she needed. By commending her, he was endorsing her ministry.

A. True
B. False

►15. The Greek word kephale/head in 1 Corinthians 11, means origin/source instead of authority/leader.

A. True
B. False

►16. In 1 Corinthians 11:5, we can see that Paul expected women to be both praying and prophesying in public worship services.

A. True
B. False

►17. "Let your women keep silence in the churches" in 1 Corinthians 14:34 teaches against women ministering publicly.

A. True
B. False

►18. Paul's three "be silents" in 1 Corinthians 14 had to do with taking turns while ministering, so that everyone would learn and be comforted.

A. True
B. False

►19. Paul agreed with the opinion of some, that it was a shame for women to speak in church.

A. True
B. False

►20. In 1 Timothy 2:11-15, Paul was instructing Timothy on how to deal with a woman who was a false teacher in the church at Ephesus. There is nothing in this passage to support the silencing of all Godly women in the church.

A. True
B. False

►21. Eve didn't become deceived because of some inherent weakness in women.

A. True
B. False

Notes:

Notes:

Notes:

www.ingramcontent.com/pod-product-compliance
Lightning Source LLC
LaVergne TN
LVHW051512080426
835509LV00017B/2034
* 9 7 8 0 9 9 0 4 3 7 6 2 8 *